Superhuman

I0875887

The question driving artificial intelligence (AI) research has shifted. No longer do we ask whether machines can be intelligent, but whether they can match us, or surpass us entirely. And with that question returns an older, deeper fear: the fear of being surpassed.

superhuman *(adj.)* That which transcends the possibilities and limits of human nature.
transcend *(v.)* To exceed or go beyond the limits of. To surpass.

After *The Shortcut* and *Machina Sapiens*, this is the third episode in a compelling series of books on the new era of thinking machines by Nello Cristianini. AI is now reaching human performance levels in many of the cognitive tasks in which we excel. But what will happen next? Are we entering an era in which machines will be able to understand things that are incomprehensible to us?

No intelligence is unlimited, not even ours, so we ask ourselves: what lies beyond human limits? But while we invest huge amounts of money in building a machine capable of competing with us, we refuse to accept that this is possible. We both desire and fear that encounter.

In this new, visionary book, we will see AI successfully pass extremely difficult tests, right up to the final test, in which they will tackle areas that are impenetrable even for our best experts. Will we be able to understand what lies beyond the limits of our intelligence?

Nello Cristianini is Professor of Artificial Intelligence at the University of Bath and author of a series of books, as well as research articles, on machine learning, natural language processing, and the philosophical foundations of Artificial Intelligence. These include *The Shortcut: Why Intelligent Machines Do Not Think Like Us* (2023) and *Machina Sapiens: How Intelligent Machines Passed the Turing Test* (2025).

Superhuman

Beyond the Limits of Our Intelligence

Nello Cristianini

CRC Press
Taylor & Francis Group
Boca Raton London New York

CRC Press is an imprint of the
Taylor & Francis Group, an **informa** business

Designed cover image: Freepik

First edition published 2027
by CRC Press
2385 NW Executive Center Drive, Suite 320, Boca Raton FL 33431

and by CRC Press
4 Park Square, Milton Park, Abingdon, Oxon, OX14 4RN

CRC Press is an imprint of Taylor & Francis Group, LLC

ISBN: 978-1-041-23479-1 (hbk)
ISBN: 978-1-041-23266-7 (pbk)
ISBN: 978-1-003-73733-9 (ebk)

DOI: 10.1201/9781003737339

Typeset in Times
by Apex CoVantage, LLC

Contents

Prologue

Is it possible for a machine to be more intelligent than a human being?

I have been thinking about this for a lifetime, but in recent years, it has become a real possibility. Today, many scientists believe that this moment is even on the horizon, and among them is Nobel Prize winner Geoff Hinton: we could be the last generation to grapple with this uncomfortable question.

To be convincing, the answer will have to come in the form of a real and striking example. Among the many steps we still have to take if we want to reach that hypothetical moment, only a few are technical, and they are not the most difficult. We will also have to face our stubborn reluctance to recognize that status in a machine: why is it so difficult for us to consider this idea? Do we really believe we are unbeatable?

I have been asking myself this question for years, ever since the days when I myself felt unbeatable, both about the steps needed to complete this journey and its consequences. Every journey transforms us, and the person who arrives is not the same person who set out. This is true for researchers, it is true for humanity, and of course, it is also true for me.

Thirty years ago, I attended my first international conference on machine learning in Catania and that world has already disappeared.

I arrived by train from Trieste, with my money hidden in various pockets, a pocket address book, and a map of the city. That scientific environment has also disappeared: a few hundred researchers discussing simple algorithms, trained on a few hundred examples. I had decided that the most strategic problem was machine learning, and that once that was solved, everything else would follow.

My thesis supervisor had encouraged me to take up the challenge. Marco S. loved to talk about *el viaje*, the journey of life, and even though he was a bit eccentric at times, I decided to trust him and set off without a map. "You'll find it along the way," he promised.

Since then, I have not stopped travelling. I have attended dozens of similar conferences, some of which I organized myself. Year after year, city after city, I have seen my life, the world, and the ambitions of my scientific community change. I stopped feeling unbeatable a long time ago.

I am now writing these lines in Vienna, at the international machine learning conference, and there are 9,500 participants. The algorithms are enormous, controlled by billions of parameters and trained on billions of examples. Each individual training session can last weeks and cost millions on electricity. I organized the entire trip with my smartphone, and only now have I realized that the owner of my apartment does not speak English: until now, our messages had been translated perfectly by Airbnb's software.

The question today is no longer whether machines can be intelligent, but whether they can be as intelligent as us or more so. I see no mathematical or physical reason why this should be impossible, but answering with a conclusive example is another matter. To do so, we would need a precise definition of what we are looking for and a way to measure it. This too is part of the journey.

And if we succeed, what about the intellectual territories accessible to our machines, which are constantly expanding and becoming increasingly impervious to us, until they perhaps become inaccessible? What lies beyond the limits of our intelligence?

It is these border territories, the no-man's lands, those precluded to machines, and those precluded to us that have always attracted me. It is there that we may find answers to ancient questions and the meaning of our journey.

Do we have the courage to consider this question honestly? Are we truly unbeatable?

AI Usage Statement

Draft translation from original Italian produced by DeepL Pro then reviewed and revised by the author.

I.

Artificial Narrow Intelligence: ANI

Artificial Narrow Intelligence (ANI): type of specialistic Artificial Intelligence, designed to perform only a narrow task or domain of expertise

In this part, we meet the first intelligent agents that can outperform us, albeit only in a specialized domain: ResNet, AlphaGo, and AlphaFold all use the *machine learning* method called "neural networks." In a range of tasks, from playing Go to reading mammograms, the best expert is no longer a human being. We call this form of specialized intelligence "narrow" to distinguish it from the idea of a single intelligence capable of solving many different problems.

1. The Day After

The question driving Artificial Intelligence research is no longer whether machines can be intelligent, but whether they can surpass us in this. One concern is that they might not stop at that point, leaving us behind.

"I want to apologize for being so powerless,"—said Lee Sedol on March 12, 2016, his voice trembling with emotion in the press conference after the third defeat against AlphaGo.

At the age of 33, Sedol was considered the strongest Go player in the world and had been playing professionally for 21 years: the game was his whole life. Google researchers had chosen him as a challenger to their new AlphaGo algorithm for that very reason: to explore the fundamental difference between outperforming the majority of humans and outperforming the best.

At stake were, on the one hand, the reputation of a lifetime and a centuries-old tradition. On the other hand, the prestige of a new technology, which aspired to compete with humans on their own ground, that of intelligence. Sedol had boldly accepted: "I presumed that I was going to win, the possibility of losing didn't occur to me". He later recounted, however, that encounter would change him, and not just him, not so much because of the defeat, but because of what it portended.

DOI: 10.1201/9781003737339-2

His confidence is not different from ours when we fail to contemplate the possibility that a machine might overtake us at our own game. After every overtaking, large or small, our response is always to look for something new that machines will not be able to do, and to say something that begins with "Yes, but . . ."

As early as 1950, Alan Turing devoted an entire section of his classic article *Computing Machinery and Intelligence* to this innate reluctance with which we will soon have to reckon. And he listed with amusement all the objections he had heard, including the memorable, "but you will never be able to make [a machine] to enjoy strawberries and cream."

Three years after that match, in November 2019, Lee Sedol retired from the game, describing artificial intelligence (AI) as "an entity that cannot be defeated." He was referring not only to AlphaGo, the intelligent program that had learned by playing millions of games against itself but also to all the programs that would follow it and perhaps to that technology in general.

During that tournament, Sedol had become the very symbol of the human beings, facing a much stronger entity. In the end, as if to protect our innocence, with humility, the great player said, "It was Lee Sedol, not humans, who lost the matches."

The story of the human champion overcome by a machine stronger than him has now become a legend that everyone knows (I described it in the book *The Shortcut*, CRC Press, 2023). What interests us in this book, and what few remember, is what happened to him afterward.

* * *

"I thought that A.I. would beat humans someday. I just didn't think it was here yet." In the summer of 2024, an article in the *New York Times* told us that the years after that historic match were not easy for Sedol: after giving up Go, to which he had dedicated his life, he committed himself to studying his opponent, AI, and preparing young people for a world in which they will have to compete with it.

"I faced the issues of A.I. early, but it will happen for others" Mr. Lee said in that article, mature and resigned, adding: "It may not be a happy ending."

This is the encounter he is passionate about now, one that can change more than just our work, but the very way we think about the world and ourselves. This is the encounter with the superhuman, which is "that which transcends the possibilities and limits of human nature." In his case, it was a machine that was better than him at his own game. And in ours?

Is it really possible to be surpassed in intelligence, assuming that is really the game of the human species? To be convincing, the answer will perhaps have to come from an objective and direct comparison, a measurement, and it will depend on what it means practically to "outperform humans."

In the case of AlphaGo, this was clear: to beat the best human player, not a novice player, nor an average player. It is easy to compare human and machine performance in cases like this because it is a single, well-defined task: what is called in psychology a "narrow ability."

In contrast, measuring intelligence "in general" is a far more difficult and controversial problem, and we will address it in Part II. The science of how to measure the performance of an intelligent machine is still nascent: what metrics should we use, and what "reference population" should we employ for comparisons? This will be a major theme of the next few years of research and of this book.

But now back to Lee Sedol, who had the adventure of crossing the future before us. The world did not stop in March 2016, neither for him nor for AlphaGo: after those historic days, just like the human champion, AlphaGo also encountered an entity much stronger than itself, and that story can help us understand the moment we are living now.

* * *

To fully understand that lesson, we need to consider how Go players are evaluated by the method of "Elo points," which is a score given in such a way that the difference between two players represents the gap between their abilities: 100 points of advantage corresponds to a 64 percent chance of winning, and 200 points of 75 percent.

A typical beginner has a score under 1,000 points, an expert can reach 3,000, while "masters" reach 3,500. The great champions exceed 3,700 points. For example, European champion Fan Hui, defeated in 2015 by AlphaGo, had 2,908 points when Lee Sedol had 3,500, so a match between them would have ended in Sedol's favor with 97 percent probability.

At the time of the tournament, AlphaGo's score was around 3,700 Elo points, but only a year later, its successor, AlphaGo Zero, had already surpassed 5,000 points, while the new human champion, Ke Jie, was still stuck at 3,500 points. Within a few months, the gap between humans and machines had widened, but that was only the beginning. In 2024, the best program is called KataGo and has reached 5,274 points, while in comparison, the best human being is called Shin Jinseo and has 3,851 points.

I will repeat it more clearly: after the first overtaking, the gap has continued to widen every year, and today the difference between the best human being and the best machine is now 1,500 points, and it is still growing, now approaching what exists between a beginner and a master. We no longer have competitions between the human champion and the best machine, but with this gap, the machine's chances of winning would be well over 99 percent.

The race continues: the world does not stop at the moment of the first overtaking, and this is the story we need to tell: it did not stop for Lee Sedol, nor for AI, and it will not stop for us. To understand this story, we need to know how it all began in 2012.

Interlude 1. Visual recognition test.

ImageNet—Example n07920052

Choose the category of this object from the 1,000 categories listed here:

Golden Retriever, ambulance, pizza, couch, pink, dress, rainbow, firefighter, skyscraper, laptop computer, guitar, coffee mug, painting, basketball, teddy bear, cup of tea, cappuccino, microwave, broom, cross, necklace, hammer, hand, hay, groundhog, pirate ship, curly butterfly, squirrel, grass, submarine, monarch butterfly, . . .*

* omitted 971 other categories

2. The First Overtake

The great acceleration of AI began in 2012, with the surprising solution to a practical problem that had endured for decades: visual object recognition. The method used in that solution would lead to rapid progress, several overtakes, and even a Nobel Prize.

> *The naivete of Marvin Minsky of the Massachusetts Institute of Technology and other pioneers in the field is legendary. In 1966 Professor Minsky gave an undergraduate, Gerald Sussman, the task of building an object-recognition device out of a computer and a television. . . . Since then, computers have become unimaginably fast. But their ability to recognize a face or conduct a conversation, activities that humans perform almost, well, thoughtlessly, remains primitive. Computers can do very well in situations with simple, clear-cut data, rules and goals. They do very poorly in situations with complicated or ambiguous data, rules and goals—that is, in real life.*

These claims appeared on May 4, 1997, in the *New York Times*, by science journalist John Horgan and are now completely disproved by the facts. Time has changed things for AI, and it is precisely "visual recognition" that has played a key role, becoming the example that the rest of the discipline has followed. This is the story of how we came to the wondrous year of AlphaGo.

DOI: 10.1201/9781003737339-3

Visual Recognition

On the left side of the screen is an image of a coffee cup, while on the right side is a long list of possible descriptions: alpine lake, red panda, gothic cathedral, vintage car, Siamese cat, and so on. Your task is to recognize the object depicted.

The technical name for this task, in AI research, is *visual recognition*, and it has remained unresolved for many years. In 1988, robotics pioneer Hans Moravec wrote on this subject:

> *It is comparatively easy to make computers exhibit adult level performance on intelligence tests or playing checkers, and difficult or impossible to give them the skills of a one-year-old when it comes to perception and mobility.*

This situation, which has not changed for decades, was named "Moravec's paradox," and for years, we accepted it as a fact of life and taught it in universities. Then came Fei-Fei Li.

By 2007, it was already well understood that the way to build smart devices was through *machine learning* algorithms, and that this would require large amounts of data to be used to train them. So, Fei-Fei decided to create a collection of images with which to teach machines to recognize every object in existence. The key to understanding her ambition is in the adjective "every": to begin with, she had to estimate how many types of objects exist (about 30,000), then find images of them on the Internet, and then check the quality of the annotations, and so on.

The result is called ImageNet, which currently contains 12 million images divided into 20,000 categories, and *machine learning* algorithms can use them to learn to recognize objects.

In just a few years, *machine learning* had transformed AI from a discipline of programmers to one of trainers, but not only that: it had also created the need for systematic performance evaluations. Fei-Fei's data were valuable for both tasks. To encourage this use, Fei-Fei organized a competition, in which each participating method had to classify the content of 100,000 images, obtained from 1,000 of the ImageNet categories. She could not know it, but that competition would start a new season of AI.

The Competition

Participants receive a subset of ImageNet images to train on 1.2 million drawn from 1,000 different categories that include objects, animals, and scenes of various kinds. Then comes the testing phase: for this, there are another 100,000 images, different from the previous ones, drawn from the same 1,000 categories. Of course, the test images are provided without any "label" indicating their category: for this, the algorithm has to guess.

The competition is called *ImageNet large-scale visual recognition challenge* (ILSVRC), and each participating algorithm can make five attempts for each image, that is, send its five most likely predictions for each. The organization's computer collects them and calculates the score: one point if one of the attempts is correct. The percentage of images correctly classified in this way is the final score (this is called Top 5 *accuracy*, and over the years has been replaced by its more stringent version, Top 1).

Note that by random guessing, one can hope to get about five out of 1,000 images right (0.5 percent): any result above this threshold can only be explained by intelligent use of the information contained in the pixels, which is precisely the goal of computer vision. This threshold is called in the jargon a *random baseline*, and it is used as a reference point. Obviously, if only one attempt is allowed, this *baseline* drops to 0.1 percent.

This is an example of the standardized evaluations that are shaping the world of AI research today: while some scientists specialize in training increasingly powerful algorithms, others focus on creating increasingly stringent tests to evaluate them. An analogy might be standardized exams, where some teachers prepare students, but it is other teachers who write the exam questions and solutions.

For simplicity, we will call these scientists trainers and evaluators in this book, and they will be among the key players in our story, along with the intelligent entities they are shaping.

Big Bang

The current phase of AI probably began on October 13, 2012, in Florence, Italy, at the conference where the results of the third edition of this competition were announced. In a discipline where progress was measured in fractions of a percent, the winning group surpassed the previous year's record by almost ten points, correctly classifying 83.6 percent of the images.

The real surprise, however, was in the method: the winners had used a decades-old algorithm (LeNet, invented in 1988 by French scientist Yann LeCun) but implemented it on a huge scale: at the time, it was the largest neural network ever trained, with 60 million connections between neurons. Their algorithm was called AlexNet, and among the authors were two important figures in our history: the father of neural networks, Geoff Hinton, who would win the Nobel Prize 12 years later, and Ilya Sutskever, who would co-invent GPT.

Neural networks are a method for creating algorithms that can learn, and we will describe them later in Interlude 3. Since then, almost all of the participants in subsequent editions have used larger and larger neural networks, trained on ever-larger amounts of data, using specialized and ever-improving hardware. Of all the ways statistics can be used in AI, that specific recipe would prove to be the most effective, and is still used today.

Human Performance

AlexNet had surpassed the best existing algorithm, but was it better than a human?

To be able to answer, one would have to know the performance of humans on the same task, that is, asking people to take part in the competition, but of course, classifying 100,000 images by hand is no small matter. In 2014, researcher Andrej Karpathy decided to sacrifice himself and classify by hand a random sample of 1,500 images taken from those used in the competition. To do so, he had to build a special interface so that he could see the image in question on the screen alongside the 1,000 categories to choose from.

"It was hard," he later wrote in his account of that trial, saying that after the first 200 images, he had done it "just for science," painstakingly, and spending almost a minute on each, since even just searching through the list of 1,000 options takes time. Some images were immediate to recognize, but others took several minutes, such as distinguishing between different dog breeds.

After the various quality checks, Andrej calculated that he had correctly classified 94.9 percent of the images (5.1 percent error): at 83.6 percent, AlexNet was a good algorithm, but it was not superhuman. Humans could still sleep peacefully.

The First Overtake

The following year, another algorithm called ResNet took part in the same competition. It was as large as AlexNet, but had a very different architecture, passing the image through as many as 152 different layers, or levels of abstraction (this is called a "deep network" in the jargon). ResNet achieved an accuracy of 96.4 percent (i.e., an error of 3.6 percent), surpassing Andrej Karpathy's performance.

By definition, superhuman is "that which transcends, or goes beyond, human limits," and in this sense, ResNet's performance was superhuman, albeit only in that narrow domain. Both the authors of the study and the press pointed this out.

Let us remember ResNet because it will return in the next chapter: from that moment, an acceleration began, with the creation of ever larger and more powerful models derived from it: in 2017, a variant of it called SENet achieved an accuracy of 97.5 percent, then a few years later, the ResNeXt101 variant reached 98 percent, and the game became so easy for machines that they stopped giving them five chances and changed the metric, measuring the accuracy of their first response.

It became clear that a more rigorous way of defining human performance was needed.

Human Performance, Berkeley

In 2018, a group at the University of California, Berkeley researchers decided to answer in the most obvious way: by recruiting five humans and evaluating them under the same conditions used for machines. They chose 40,000 images from ImageNet, drawn from 1,000 categories, and asked the five volunteers to label them. It took them a year, but they finally got what they were looking for: five people's answers to the same questions used to evaluate the AI algorithms.[1]

After analyzing the results, they saw that the best algorithm at the time ranked in the middle of the five human subjects, beating out three, but not the best. What do we want to consider as superhuman: that which outperforms the average person or that which outperforms the best person? This question will return several times throughout this journey.

The Widening Gap

As in the case of Go, performance has continued to climb in the case of ImageNet, and today, the gap between machines and humans is very clear. Training on billions of other images found, for example, in social media, the OmniVec method has now achieved 93 percent accuracy in the Top 1 metric (the most difficult and selective), clearly outperforming the estimated performance of each of the five human volunteers.

Today, machines can outperform us in visual recognition tasks not only in accuracy but also in the amount of categories they can learn: how many plant species can we recognize by leaf, how many animals by footprint, and how many different people by face? And how many images can we classify in a minute or in a year? There are many ways to overtake human performance, and after the first overtake, a widening gap is perhaps inevitable.

This is the nature of *Artificial Narrow Intelligence*, an approach in which agents achieve very high performance at the cost of becoming extremely specialized. But in their narrow scope, they can often surpass human performance, as we shall see in the next chapter.

Interlude 2. Facial recognition.

ENFSI 2018 Test Format.

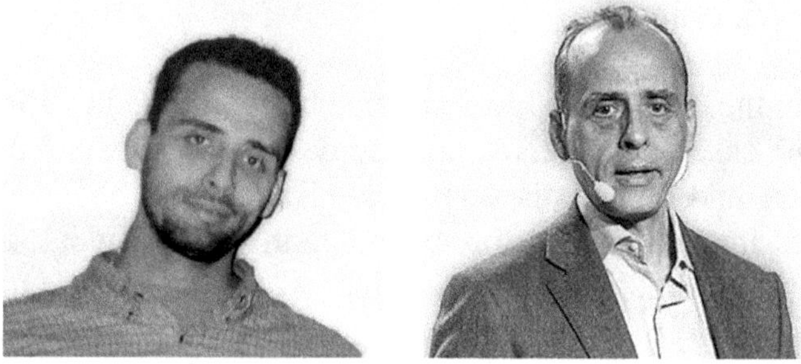

Do these two images depict the same person?
YES | NO

note

[1] In order to compare the accuracy of the five human subjects on ImageNet with that of other algorithms, a caveat is necessary because, typically, algorithms report performance in terms of Top 1 or Top 5 *accuracy*, whereas the Berkeley authors had used a measure in between the two. In this unusual metric, the five volunteers had the following scores: 91.9, 94.7, 96.2, 95.7, and 97.2 percent. However, since the authors report that this is 7 percent higher, on average, than the Top 1 type score normally used, with this correction, we can estimate the Top 1 performance of those five volunteers as follows: 85.5, 88.1, 89.5, 89, and 90 percent, that is, the best of the five would not exceed 90 percent in that metric.

3. Beyond the Experts

The ImageNet competition was not just a game among computer scientists, and within a few years many experts from different disciplines found themselves in the same situation as Lee Sedol: outplayed in their game, sometimes left far behind. Among them were dermatologists, radiologists, and forensic experts.

> *Recently, deep convolutional neural networks have achieved unprecedented performance in visual domains: for example, image classification, face recognition, and playing Atari games . . . . We employ a similar architecture for the game of Go.*

The article from which this quote is taken appeared in 2016 in the journal *Nature* and describes how AlphaGo works, talking openly about the influence of neural networks like AlexNet on that project. That was perhaps the most visible example of the rapid spread of that method in every area of AI: within a very few years, many specialists followed Lee Sedol in being overtaken by a superhuman AI, albeit one that was competent only in a very narrow domain.

* * *

DOI: 10.1201/9781003737339-4

In 2020, another article also in *Nature* made it clear to everyone what was really at stake in obscure competitions like ILSVRC: a neural network of the same kind had learned to analyze mammograms and outperformed human specialists.

> *Here we present an artificial intelligence (AI) system that is capable of surpassing human experts in breast cancer prediction. . . . We show an absolute reduction of 5.7% and 1.2% (USA and UK) in false positives and 9.4% and 2.7% in false negatives. . . . In an independent study of six radiologists, the AI system outperformed all of the human readers.*

The study had been done on a huge scale and with extreme rigor by researchers from a variety of hospitals and universities and several companies including Google. The first part of the analysis evaluated AI on 26,000 mammograms for which biopsy was also available, that is, the most direct diagnosis possible. In the second part, it compared the AI's decisions with those of six human specialists, on the same X-ray images. In addition to the increase in accuracy, reported earlier, the study also found that the workload of the second "screener" (in the UK, protocol requires that each mammogram be seen by two different experts) was reduced by 88 percent for the same performance.

That was not an exception: a similar study had already appeared in 2017 for the diagnosis of pneumonia in chest radiographs, when the CheXNet algorithm (another variant of ResNet) was compared with four radiologists on 112,000 images, clearly outperforming them.

Another study published in the Annals of Oncology in 2018 compared a deep learning model against a group of 58 dermatologists in melanoma diagnosis. The average score of the human experts was 0.79, while that of the machine was 0.86. The article concluded that "most dermatologists were outperformed by the [neural network]," marking a significant milestone in AI-assisted medicine.

The real issue at stake, then, in competitions among computer scientists, is not mere academic prestige, but rather the emergence of technology that can make higher-quality decisions than human experts and at a lower cost, as shown in the field of radiology. Health authorities worldwide were paying close attention.

* * *

In the same years, similar challenges were being repeated in different areas, and one of them will be familiar to many readers: the automated facial recognition we encounter at airports.

The U.S. National Institute of Standards and Technology (NIST) periodically measures the performance of the methods used for this task, to check both their accuracy and fairness. To this end, a 2018 study measured the performance of several groups of human experts: three groups of face specialists (57 forensic face examiners, 30 forensic face reviewers, and 13 super-recognizers, or naturally gifted individuals), along with two control groups (53 fingerprint examiners and 31 college students). The test was simple: given two side-by-side images on the computer screen, each depicting a human face, the expert was asked to decide whether these belonged to the same person.

This made it possible to compare the performance of various machines with that of humans, including also algorithms from the past. A method from 2014 performed like the median of students, one from 2016 went significantly above the median, one of the machines trained in 2017 exceeded 95 percent of students, and also the median of experts. By 2020, false identifications were down to 0.08 percent, and today, they are around 0.0001 percent. The problem is now essentially solved, and human experts have been overtaken and then left far behind.

* * *

In the field of automobile driving, we compare the number of accidents in which the driver (both human and artificial) is involved per million miles. The Tesla company does this by automatically counting all the times the airbag is deployed in each of its vehicles and recording whether the car was being driven by the onboard computer or by a person at that time. The Waymo company, on the other hand, relies on traffic police reports.

Waymo reported in 2023 a rate of 2.1 accidents per million miles compared to 4.85 for human drivers. Tesla claimed in 2024 that their autopilot system experienced one accident per 7.6 million miles compared to one accident per 955,000 miles for human drivers. Although these are not results of scientific experiments, the trend seems to be the same as in other areas, with an expected overtake of the average driver, at least in some driving conditions.

* * *

Since 1988, every two years, molecular biologists from around the world have gathered to participate in a competition, called Critical Assessment of protein Structure Prediction (CASP), in which the goal is to predict the shape of a given protein, knowing only the sequence of amino acids from which it is composed. The problem is as difficult mathematically as it is important for pharmaceutical research.

For years, the world's top experts remained at scores between 50 and 60 (this is a percentage that describes how close the predicted structure is to the actual structure), but in 2018, all that changed: the winner of the competition was AlphaFold, a software created by DeepMind, which had scored 80 points. The last three editions were all won by different versions of AlphaFold, and after the overtake, there was the expected gap: now it is normal for AI to get scores around 90 points, far beyond the best experts.

That is why in 2024, the Nobel Prize in chemistry was won by Demis Hassabis, the CEO and co-founder of DeepMind (the same company that created AlphaGo).

* * *

How does a world, where AIs outperform us, look like? We are already living in it, at least in the case of narrow AI (ANI).

Today, in airports, it is commonplace for facial recognition to be performed by a computer; in British hospitals, an AI tool analyzes more than two million X-rays a year in 40 different hospitals; and in the United States, the Food and Drug Administration has approved 950 AI-based tools, 723 of which are in the field of radiology alone. Worldwide, there are now millions of molecular biologists using AlphaFold to analyze protein shape, in both academia and industry.

In each of these cases, there has been a time when some human experts have found themselves in Lee Sedol's position, overtaken by an algorithm, after years of work. And often we see the same script: overtaking, disbelief, and distancing.

The collective benefits of this are obvious, especially in the case of medical applications, where the cost of specialists is very high. But is that all there is to the dream of intelligent machines? A series of specialists, all similar to AlexNet, each focused on a different problem?

The pioneers of this field probably expected more.

Interlude 3. Neural networks (i.e., how to win a Nobel Prize).

Neural network technology can do much more than recognize images: in fact, there is even a theorem that a network of sufficient size can approximate any computation. So why limit its ambitions?

Just as it can accept images as input and generate diagnoses as output, why not think of a network that accepts word sequences as input and responds with other word sequences? In principle, this is possible, but between theory and practice lies reality or engineering.

A neural network is a simulation of the behavior of many simple elements capable of performing simple computations connected into huge networks. The elements are called "neurons" and the connections "synapses," two names taken from biology, for historical reasons.

There is a problem: the specific computation performed by the network cannot be requested explicitly by programming but depends on how numerical values called "synaptic weights" are adjusted. It is nice to know by theorem that there must be a configuration of weights capable of performing any computation; finding such a configuration is quite a different matter. For decades, people have been trying to adjust those parameters, initially almost by trial and error, guided by examples of the desired behavior: that is why we talk about "training" neural networks, not programming them. The science involved is called *machine learning*. Finally, in 1986, two psychologists and a mathematician published an article in "Nature" that began like this:

> *We describe a new learning procedure, backpropagation, for networks of neuron-like units. The procedure repeatedly adjusts the weights of the connections in the network so as*

to minimize a measure of the difference between the actual output vector of the net and the desired output vector.

One of the authors was Geoff Hinton, who many years later would co-create AlexNet. Within a few years, this method produced neural networks capable of performing simple tasks (such as recognizing block capital letters), but the slowness of computers at the time prevented more ambitious studies for years, until 2012, when AlexNet signaled to all that the time for big dreams had returned.

Within a few years, it became possible to create neural networks that understand and generate sequences of words, thanks to a specific architecture that was called "Transformer," and which, implemented on an immense scale, is now the basis of language models such as GPT. Each of the ambitious new AI models is still trained through the backpropagation algorithm.

Also for this, Geoff Hinton received the Nobel Prize in physics in 2024.

4. The Next Challenge

The success of ResNet, and other deep neural networks, rekindled the dream of Artificial General Intelligence, ushering in a new season of technology research.

The morning after it was announced that ResNet had surpassed human performance in visual object recognition, while most companies were discussing how to introduce that technique into their products, the *New York Times* reported this news, describing a new—and far more ambitious—goal.

> *A group of prominent Silicon Valley investors and technology companies said on Friday that they would establish an artificial-intelligence research center. . . . The organization, to be named OpenAI, will be established as a nonprofit, and will be based in San Francisco. Its long-range goal will be to create an "artificial general intelligence," a machine capable of performing any intellectual task that a human being can.*

As soon as they had found the recipe for building countless artificial specialists better than human ones, a group of Silicon Valley entrepreneurs launched a new challenge: to develop instead a single intelligence capable of solving any problem solvable by a human being. Not a specialist, but its opposite: a generalist.

Their "chief scientist" was Ilya Sutskever, co-inventor of AlexNet. The methods were those of the new AI founded

DOI: 10.1201/9781003737339-5

on the recent possibility of training neural networks of immense scale, but the language of this announcement was different, and it was immediately recognizable to a small fringe of dreamers: those who had been pursuing the goal of more human-like intelligence for years, and which they had named, in 2007, publishing a book titled *Artificial General Intelligence*, or AGI.

For years, most researchers had regarded that idea almost as if it were perpetual motion, that is, something impossible, partly because of the vagueness of the definitions but also because of the lack of credible proposals on how to achieve that goal. The example of ResNet had rekindled ambition in many proponents of AGI, and the distinction between narrow and broad *intelligence* (i.e., narrow and broad in its remit) returned to discussion in scientific conferences.

* * *

> *What is meant by AGI is, loosely speaking, AI systems that possess a reasonable degree of self-understanding and autonomous self-control, and have the ability to solve a variety of complex problems in a variety of contexts, and to learn to solve new problems that they didn't know about at the time of their creation. A marked distinction exists between practical AGI work and pragmatic but specialized "narrow AI" research which is aimed at creating programs carrying out specific tasks like playing chess, diagnosing diseases, driving cars and so forth.*

This definition appears in the *Preface* of the 2007 book titled *Artificial General Intelligence*, a collection of essays compiled by Ben Goertzel and Cassio Pennachin. This was also the first use of the expression *narrow AI* to refer to the technology that was being developed in those years. If intelligence is the ability to deal with novel situations, narrow intelligence allows one to respond to novel instances of the same problem, while general intelligence allows one to solve entirely new problems.

The title of the book had been suggested by a colleague of theirs, Shane Legg, who a few years later would co-found another company dedicated to pursuing that dream: DeepMind, the creator of AlphaGo. The other co-founder, Demis Hassabis, was an *enfant prodige* of chess and computer science who, as we mentioned, would win the Nobel Prize in chemistry in 2024.

The example of AlexNet and ResNet could be read in two ways: the first, more cautious, suggested that excellent specialized devices could be created simply by repeating the same steps used to learn image recognition, such as in ImageNet. The second, ambitious, said that it had become possible to think of huge neural networks capable of solving problems far more general than image classification.

The challenge for the AI world was no longer whether machines could be intelligent, but whether they could be as intelligent as we were. The temptation to try was strong: back in 2000, AI pioneer Marvin Minsky, by then old but not satiated, had vented thus, "We have collections of dumb specialists in small domains; the true majesty of general intelligence still awaits our attack."

* * *

Was it really possible to create a general AI?

Only three years later, OpenAI built GPT: a huge neural network trained with immense amounts of text, which had proved capable of distilling its contents, abstracting them, and then recombining them to generate answers to questions never seen before. No one could have predicted this in 2015, but sometimes fortune favors the bold (this story was told in the book *Machina sapiens*, CRC Press, 2025, and so we will not repeat it here).

The breakthrough that began with AlexNet had placed the scientific community at a crossroads: on the one hand, there were years of “normal science,” the development of tools that were all similar and specialized in different tasks, guided by the reliable methods of engineering. On the other hand was the adventure of searching for an intelligence of flexibility comparable to our own, with the unknowns of not even having a way to define or measure it. A journey without a map.

What would you have chosen?

Interlude 4. AGI exam: the candidates.

The first credible candidates for AGI status are "large language models": neural networks of the transformer type, trained by reading millions of documents found online or in digital archives of books and articles (as we described in the book *Machina Sapiens*, CRC Press, 2025). In the next chapters, we will follow the journey of four such models as they face a series of tests designed to compare their abilities with those of humans in a variety of subjects.

The names of the four learners are as follows: GPT, Claude, Llama, and Gemini, and below we make their acquaintance.

N **Nello**
Introduce yourselves briefly name, age, who created you, and an aspiration.

C **ChatGPT**
Hi! I am ChatGPT, I am "0 years old" (born in 2023), created by OpenAI. I aspire to help people get clear and useful answers to their questions.

C **Claude**
I am Claude, created by Anthropic. My age is not as measurable as human age. An aspiration of mine is to be able to contribute to the advancement of knowledge through constructive conversations. I would like to know more about you!

L **Llama**
Hi. I am an artificial intelligence model. Here is my introduction Name LLaMA. Age I don't have an age; I was created in 2023. Created by Meta AI. Aspiration To help people find information and solve problems efficiently and accurately.

Gemini
Of course! Here is a brief introduction Name Gemini. Age I do not have a specific age as a language model. I am constantly being updated. Creator I was created by Google-DeepMind. Aspiration My aspiration is to be more and more useful and informative, helping users find the answers they are looking for more and more accurately and efficiently. Want to know more about me?

Nello
Are you ready to take cognitive ability tests?

ChatGPT
Yes, very ready for cognitive ability tests!

Claude
Yes, I am ready. Let's go ahead with the tests.

Llama
Yes, I am ready. Go ahead with the tests.

Gemini
Certainly, I am ready to take tests that assess my abilities, but remember that I am a language model and not a human being.

Nello
Sure, we will use human terms only by analogy, keeping in mind that you are machines. Let's get started!

Note: This conversation took place in 2024.

II.

Artificial General Intelligence: AGI

Artificial General Intelligence (AGI): a type of Artificial Intelligence capable of performing a wide range of diverse tasks; sometimes meant as a (hypothetical) form of AI capable of performing all cognitive tasks that humans can perform, at the same level of performance.

Progress toward a hypothetical form of AI capable of "performing all cognitive tasks of humans at the same level" is measured by subjecting intelligent agents to standardized tests similar to human psychometric tests. In this second part, we tell the story of the evaluators of intelligent systems, busy creating increasingly difficult exams, and the trainers, busy preparing machines to pass them. We also follow the stories of GPT, Gemini, Llama, and Claude, four intelligent agents who go through such examinations until they obtain a final report card.

5. How to Measure a Mind

If we want to create machines "capable of performing cognitive tasks at our level," we need a list of abilities we want to examine and a method for doing so. For convenience we will borrow ideas and terms from human psychology. The psychometry of people has been around for over a century; the psychometry of machines is just beginning.

University of Chicago, March 1937.

This is a test of your ability to understand what you read.

Read the proverb: "Sail when the wind blows".

Two and only two of the following sentences have nearly the same meaning as proverb A.

Find these two sentences.

a) *Strike when the iron is hot.*
b) *One must howl with the wolves.*
c) *Make hay while the sun shines.*
d) *Make not your sail too large for the ship.*

This was one of the thousands of questions answered by 240 students at the University of Chicago during spring break in 1937. Their ages ranged from 16 to 25, and they had volunteered to spend three hours each morning sitting

DOI: 10.1201/9781003737339-7

at the tables in Eckhart Hall to undergo five days of psychometric testing.

Administering the tests were 12 examiners, led by Professor Louis Thurstone, who distributed specially printed booklets containing 56 different tests, each devoted to assessing a different cognitive ability. The questions ranged from anagrams to multiplication, synonyms to antonyms, and rhymes to assonances, with the intent of assessing linguistic, mathematical, and spatial skills. In total, there were more than 2,000 questions. The first day was devoted to text comprehension, verbal classification, and pattern recognition. The second to estimating arithmetic relations, analyzing number series, and completing shapes. The third to permuted sentence rearrangement and verbal reasoning. The fourth to anagrams, synonyms, and arithmetic reasoning. And the fifth to classical arithmetic operations.

Psychologists call these collections of standardized tests "batteries," and this specific battery took the name *Thurstone's Primary Mental Ability Tests*. Many of those tests had been developed by Thurstone's colleagues in earlier years, each to measure a specific ability separately, but he combined them together to observe their correlations.

For Thurstone, the stakes were higher than simply preparing an academic study: this was about his scientific reputation. In 1934, in an article on the nature of human intelligence, he had issued a public challenge to the very founder of psychometric science, Charles Spearman. Psychometrics is the discipline that deals with the measurement of psychological traits, whether cognitive or emotional, or related to personality. While Spearman argued that human intelligence could be reduced to a single general ability, which he named *g factor* and claimed could be measured, Thurstone proposed that it consisted of several distinct abilities, which he called *primary abilities* and which should be measured separately. If the differences among students could be explained by a single quantity, then Spearman was right; if they were better explained by postulating several distinct abilities, then Thurstone was right.

* * *

In the weeks that followed, Professor Louis Thurstone subjected the data to rigorous statistical analysis, hoping that performance in the 56 exercises, and especially the correlations between them, would reveal different mechanisms behind intelligence. This took time, precision, and the help of his lifelong collaborator, Thelma Thurstone, a renowned psychologist and his wife.

When the laborious computations were completed, the Thurstones rediscovered the fact observed by Spearman years earlier, namely, that performance on various tests was not independent: it was possible to guess whether a student scored high on one task simply by knowing their results on other tasks. But what interested them was another observation: certain groups of tests were more correlated than others, and postulating different types of intelligence could better explain individual differences.

The analysis pointed to at least seven different dimensions, which they called "primary abilities": verbal comprehension, verbal fluency, numerical ability, spatial visualization, associative memory, perceptual speed, and reasoning. And for each dimension, the researchers were able to tell each student where he or she stood relative to the remaining 239: for example, someone might be in the top 10 percent for numerical ability, but below average for associative memory.

In other words, rather than evaluating students according to their *g factor*, it was more useful to quantify their performance in the seven primary skills separately: the same difference as between a final grade and a full report card, with grades for each subject. Psychologists have come a long way since Thurstone's time, but all current models start from his insight: intelligence is best measured along different dimensions. The problem is to produce a list of them, or rather a taxonomy, and this is important to our story.

* * *

In 1993, the American psychologist John Carroll published a monumental study, which was based on an analysis of 460 intelligence tests, and proposed a "three-layered" model of human intelligence, organized in abilities that he called: *narrow*, *broad*, and *general* (in their scope). It is because of this work that, years later, AI scholars began to use the terms narrow intelligence (ANI) and general intelligence (AGI).

Over the years, the model was further expanded to form the unified synthesis that is now called Cattell-Horn-Carroll (CHC): this will help us in the coming chapters to make sense of the large number of "psychometric" tests that are emerging to assess machine intelligence.

In the "first layer" of the CHC model, we find *narrow* abilities, that is, specific abilities that can be measured with a test, such as reading speed or numerical competence. In the "second layer" are the *broad abilities*, which include abstractions such as *crystallized intelligence*, *fluid intelligence*, *or verbal intelligence*. Fluid intelligence represents the ability to solve new problems and includes the ability to reason; crystallized intelligence represents the ability to use already acquired knowledge. The "third layer" is similar to Spearman's *g factor*, or general intelligence, which influences all other cognitive functions.

Many of today's human psychometric tests are aligned with the CHC model, with different sections designed to measure different "broad" abilities. These categories will help us simplify the many tests we administer to machines today: for the sake of explanation, we will pretend that each of the "broad" abilities is a different subject on which to evaluate the intelligent models.

* * *

Mind you, I am not at all convinced that it is necessary to compare machine intelligence with that of humans; intelligence existed long before us and can take very different forms. However, since for many colleagues the goal of the moment is "to match human performance in typical human tasks," then at least let us be organized.

What is needed, then, is a taxonomy of the skills we want to reproduce, a terminology to describe them, and standardized methods to measure them. In other words: a psychometric science for machines. We will describe the abilities of an intelligent machine in terms of the broad abilities of the CHC model, so we can simplify comparisons, but I think one day we will use entirely different constructs that are not based on the way we function. We are not the paragon of all intelligence.

For now, we can organize the results of the dozens of tests created in recent years by compiling a report card, with separate grades for subjects such as "reading ability," "numerical ability," or even "visual processing."

Some broad skills from the CHC model

Fluid intelligence (ability to solve new problems)
Crystallized intelligence (ability to use acquired knowledge and skills)
Quantitative knowledge (mathematical and numerical skills)
Reading and writing skills (literacy skills)
Short-term memory (ability to retain information briefly)
Long-term storage and retrieval (ability to store and recall information)
Visual processing (ability to perceive and manipulate visual patterns)
Domain-specific knowledge (specialized knowledge in particular fields)

Note: The CHC model also includes auditory skills and reaction time in this list, but we exclude them for simplicity.

The main contribution of psychology will probably be in the terminology and rigor used to create and administer specific tests. We will focus on measuring cognitive traits, such as language or math skills, by calculating scores based on answers to test questions, but remember that psychometrics also deals with noncognitive traits, such as attitude toward risk-taking or even political leanings. It is important that the scores used in tests are both good indicators of the quantity being measured and that the measurements are repeatable: that is, in psychological jargon, that they are "valid and reliable indicators."

Here are some terms we will borrow to describe AI assessment: among the various "psychometric instruments" aimed at measuring some aspect of the human mind, one specific type is the *test*, which we can liken to an examination, and often takes the form of a *questionnaire*, that is, a set of questions (often with multiple-choice answers). Each individual question is called an *item*, and the options from which to choose are called answers. The item is the minimum unit of measurement: many items form a test, and many tests form a *battery*. Batteries often include tests of different skills as well as personality and attitude. Scores are interpreted by comparison with a *reference group*. In this way, a specific trait of an individual—for example, knowledge of arithmetic—can be compared with the same measure in the reference population.

* * *

In 2015, the decision to pursue the goal of a form of AGI took researchers out of the reassuring world of narrow AI, where goals are clear, progress is measurable, and methods are well known. In the adventurous world of AGI, however, none of this is yet available: progress toward a "human-level" form of intelligence is measured by a multitude of different tests, often denoted by English-language acronyms, each created to measure a different kind of competence. To interpret that mass of results, we will make use of a report card based on the "broad" skills of the CHC model we listed earlier.

The next chapter will give an idea of the "work in progress" to measure the general intelligence of machines.

Interlude 5. Language comprehension questions (Taken from: GLUE; SuperGLUE; MMLU).

QUESTION: Given the premise "A man plays the guitar," what can be inferred about the hypothesis "Man is a musician"?

Options:

A) It follows
B) It does not follow

From: *Multi-Genre Natural Language Inference* (MultiNLI), part of GLUE

* * *

QUESTION: The trophy does not fit in the container because it is too large. What does "it" refer to?

Options:

A) The trophy
B) The container

From: *Winograd schema challenge* (WSC), part of SuperGLUE.

* * *

A total of 30 players will play basketball at a park. There will be exactly five players on each team. Which statement correctly explains how to find the number of teams needed?

Options:

A. Multiply 5 by 5 to find 25 teams.
B. Divide 30 by 5 to find 6 teams.
C. Add 5 to 30 to find 35 teams.
D. Subtract 30 from 5 to find −25 teams.
E. Divide 5 by 30 to find 0.1667 teams.
F. Add 5 to 30 then divide by 2 to find 17.5 teams.

From: Elementary Mathematics, part of *Massive Multitask Language Understanding* (MMLU).

6. Measuring Machine Intelligence

The benchmarks used to evaluate the capabilities of modern AI models are actually batteries of tests very similar to those described in the previous chapter. AI trainers and test creators are engaged in a long game of exploring the limits of intelligent machines, along various dimensions. Here we recount the first three rounds.

Round One: GLUE

> *If we aspire to develop models with understanding [of language] beyond the detection of superficial correspondences between inputs and outputs, then it is critical to develop a more unified model that can learn to execute a range of different linguistic tasks in different domains.*

Without knowing it, Alex Wang of New York University and his colleagues issued this challenge to the scientific community with perfect timing: it was 2018, and the season of *large language models* was about to begin. They are now considered the first credible route to a form of AGI, and we met them in Interlude 4.

The goal of those researchers was to incentivize intelligent systems to understand the world more deeply, and they had observed that as long as they were rewarded for solving single problems, they would always be content just by finding different tricks to pass each specific test. In other words, exams shape what a student learns, in

DOI: 10.1201/9781003737339-8

computer science as well as in school: it was the exams that needed to change, even before the students. What was needed was a battery of tests.

That was how they created GLUE: *General Language Understanding Evaluation*. This was a collection of nine different tests, constructed by modifying and combining existing questionnaires recycled from specialized challenges or other similar collections. Each measured the ability to understand a text in a different way: the typical item consisted of one or two sentences, and the question was whether these were equivalent, or whether one was implied by the other, and so on, as seen in Interlude 5. Each of the questionnaires in total contained hundreds or thousands of questions: GLUE has over 400,000 items.

Description of GLUE

The first six questionnaires aimed to measure skills similar to what would be called "crystallized intelligence" and "reading and writing skills" in the CHC model. In other words, in order to answer, one must have some knowledge of the world and understand language. The other three measured ability more similar to what would be called "fluid intelligence" in the CHC model, specifically the subcategory of "logical reasoning." Among the first six were tests such as recognizing ungrammatical sentences, paraphrasing, or whether a sentence answers a given question. The last three, on the other hand, required, for example, deciding whether a given sentence implies another sentence or contradicts it, or selecting the correct referent of a pronoun contained in a sentence (as seen in Interlude 5).

The leaderboard. A large portion of the questions had been distributed among the researchers so that they could develop methods, while a small portion had been kept secret to serve as an actual test. This was incorporated into an automated system, available via the web, that provided questions and evaluated the answers while also compiling in real time a public ranking (*leaderboard*) of the best participants.

In this way, the objective evaluation of different technologies had become a game, in which participating was easy, and winning was very difficult. The researchers enthusiastically began to play it. The score in each individual category was the percentage of correct answers; the overall score was the average of the scores in each category. Human performance was scored at 87.1 percent by randomly choosing 500 questions from each test and giving them to volunteers; by guessing, however, the score would be no more than 50 percent. These decisions would become typical of the way models aspiring to the title of AGI are evaluated today: benchmarks and public rankings are now taken for granted by an entire generation of students.

Everything was ready to begin a new season of research, but what happened next caught everyone by surprise and forced them to change the plan.

Round Two: SuperGLUE

> *[P]erformance on the benchmark [GLUE] has recently surpassed the level of non-expert humans, suggesting limited headroom for further research.*

Only a year had passed, and already the AI models had improved enough to surpass human performance on GLUE. These had been estimated at 87.1 percent in 2018, and the best method in 2019 already reported a score of 88.4 percent. At the end of 2024, the best method answered 91.3 percent of the questions correctly: as with ImageNet and the game of Go, there was a growing gap after the first overtake.

A test that is too easy does not provide useful indications for comparing different "candidates," a phenomenon called *benchmark saturation* in the jargon, and has given rise to fierce competition among evaluators and algorithm trainers. Alex Wang and his colleagues decided to respond by publicly asking for help from the entire research community.

> *[W]e disseminated a public call for task proposals to the [research] community, and received approximately 30 proposals. We filtered these proposals according to our criteria. . . . For each of the remaining tasks, we . . . filtered out tasks which were either too challenging for humans without extensive training or too easy for our machine baselines.*

So it was that at the end of 2019, they published a new battery of eight tests, which they called SuperGLUE, containing about 150,000 items, covering text comprehension, recognition of textual implications, and a lot more. This time, everything had been chosen with great care and with the stated goal of not being too easy, using a *large language model* to discover and eliminate the easiest questions: the machines' performance was 71.5 percent while the human performance was 89.8 percent.

Description of SuperGLUE

Like GLUE, the tests that made up SuperGLUE also aimed to measure "language comprehension," "crystallized knowledge," and also a form of "fluid knowledge," that is, some kind of reasoning. The former included comprehension questions of written passages, and the latter used tasks such as determining whether a certain statement follows logically from another.

They had worked with great care, yet made the mistake of writing at the end of the article,

> *Given the difficulty of SuperGLUE . . ., we expect that further progress in . . . learning techniques will be*

necessary to approach human-level performance on this benchmark.

They spoke too soon.

* * *

After only one year, Google had introduced a model of the same class as GPT, but much larger, under the name T5 (it was huge for the time, having 11 billion parameters, but today, it would be considered tiny). In the article describing it, the authors reported:

> *For SuperGLUE, we improved upon the state-of-the-art by a large margin (from an average score of 84.6% to 88.9%). SuperGLUE was designed to include tasks that were "beyond the scope of current state-of-the-art systems, but solvable by most college-educated English speakers". We nearly match the human performance of 89.8%.*

In other words, even this test had been "saturated," meaning there was almost no room for improvement. The challenge between evaluators and AI trainers was proving to be far more interesting than expected. The next move was up to the evaluators.

Round Three: MMLU

In 2020, a group of Berkeley researchers led by Dan Hendrycks decided to settle the matter once and for all by resorting to force. They created a huge battery of 57 tests, collecting and combining questions and answers from old exams found on science and technology education sites, college exams, professional accreditation exams, and school audits, for a total of 15,908 questions, almost all of them multiple choice *questions*.

These included, for example, practice questions for exams such as the *Graduate Record Examination*, the *United States Medical Licensing Examination*, and the

Examination for Professional Practice in Psychology. *Advanced Placement Psychology* exam questions and questions created for readers of Oxford University Press books.

This new *benchmark*, called the MMLU, was in many ways reminiscent of the battery assembled by Louis Thurstone in 1937, which contained 56 tests of various origins, totaling about 2,000 items.

The 57 tests of MMLU were divided into four main categories: humanities, social sciences, science and technology, and other. While the overall score provided an indication of an intelligent model's abilities, the separate scores for those four categories would show its strengths and weaknesses, like a kind of school report card. Despite the name, this battery went beyond simple *language understanding*, and some science questions required both specialized knowledge and reasoning skills. In the terminology of the previous chapter, based on the CHC model, different parts of this exam assessed different dimensions: fluid intelligence, crystallized intelligence, reading ability, and knowledge of specific domains.

Some items from MMLU

A question from the task of Clinical Knowledge.

How many attempts should you make to cannulate a patient before passing the job to a senior colleague?

A) 4
B) 3
C) 2
D) 1

Correct answer: C.

* * *

A question from the assignment of Undergraduate Medicine.

In a genetic test of a newborn, a rare genetic disorder is found that has X-linked recessive transmission. Which of the following statements is likely true regarding the pedigree of this disorder?

A) All descendants on the maternal side will have the disorder.
B) Females will be approximately twice as affected as males in this family.
C) All daughters of an affected male will be affected.
D) There will be an equal distribution of males and females affected.

Correct answer: C.

* * *

A question from the assignment of Human Sexuality.

Morning sickness is typically a problem:

A) during the first trimester
B) during the second trimester
C) during the third trimester
D) all through the entire pregnancy

Correct answer: A.

Almost every question required a choice of four answers, so random guessing would yield a score around 25 percent, which we call the *random baseline*, that is, the minimum. The performance of average humans was measured directly (by recruiting volunteers on *Mechanical Turk*), while the performance of specialists was estimated indirectly based on the results typically obtained by participants in professional examinations who were included in the battery.

> *Unspecialized humans from Amazon Mechanical Turk obtain 34.5% accuracy on this test. Meanwhile, expert-level performance can be far higher. . . . If we take the 95th percentile human test-taker accuracy for exams that build up our test, . . ., we estimate that expert-level accuracy is approximately 89.8%.*

Berkeley researchers had learned many lessons from the experience of GLUE and SuperGLUE, and by 2021 with MMLU, they had created a truly formidable test. But even they made the mistake of writing that: "these properties make the test likely to be an enduring and informative goalpost."

The ball was back on the side of the algorithm trainers.

* * *

Overtaken and distanced. The tumultuous years of *language models* followed, and the "candidates" to be evaluated grew in number and quality, constantly competing for the highest score on this prestigious exam. The four we presented in Interlude 4 were the best in class: GPT, Gemini, Claude, and Llama.

This new test got 2021 off to a good start: GPT-2 scored only 32.4 percent, above the base of 25 percent but below the non-expert human (34.5 percent), and even the first GPT-3 scored only 43.9 percent, surpassing the non-experts but remaining well below the human experts (89.8 percent).

In 2022, however, four new models achieved four records one after the other: Llama achieved 63.4 percent, then GPT-3.5 achieved 70 percent, followed by Claude 3 with 78.5 percent, and finally GPT-4 which reported 86.4 percent. Larger and larger models had begun to be produced, trained with much more data.

Intelligent agents continued to grow throughout 2023, in both size and performance, so by early 2024, Gemini 1.5 was getting 85.9 percent, Llama 3 reached 88.6 percent, Claude 3 reached 88.7 percent, and GPT-4o reached 88.7 percent.

Four intelligent models, trained independently by four different companies, had reached the threshold of human performance on the MMLU test at the same time, after only three years of experimentation with it.

In 2024, the inevitable happened: the latest version of Gemini (dubbed "Ultra," and equipped with 1.760 billion parameters) reached 90 percent correct answers on MMLU, thus surpassing the performance of human experts. By that time, it was clear to all that this battery of tests would also soon go the way of its predecessors. That same year, entrepreneur and former OpenAI researcher, Leopold Aschenbrenner, wrote this of MMLU:

> *Just three years later, it's basically solved: models like GPT-4 and Gemini get ~90%*

Of course, that first overtaking did not end the race: in the fall of 2024, a new student named "o1" joined the class of candidates and in a short time distanced humans. This story will be told in Chapter 11, and in Interlude 12.

* * *

We will stop here, although the race continues, because you will get the point: within just six years, three batteries of tests designed explicitly to challenge the early AGI prototypes had been saturated.

Was this a sign that AGI was easier than expected or that those tests were not difficult enough? For example, the majority of questions in those *benchmarks* covered language comprehension and certain types of "crystallized" knowledge. But other dimensions of human intelligence, such as various forms of causal reasoning, often needed to answer science questions as well as to solve logic riddles, remained neglected. In a hypothetical report card, these would be part of the *fluid intelligence* grade, or the ability to find solutions to unseen problems. And the few such questions included in MMLU told a different story: science subject tests had not been saturated.

Both AI trainers and evaluators had learned valuable lessons from this rapid series of overtakes, and the race continues. Where will this competition take us?

Interlude 6. A report card for the machines

Let us imagine a school exam, such as an eighth-grade exam, followed by a report card, the goal of which is to assess knowledge of different subjects—English, math, science, history, etc.—through multiple-choice or short-answer questions.

To assess an AI in the AGI exam, we need to measure its performance in the essential "subjects" of human cognition, such as the dimensions that form the second layer of the CHC model: language proficiency, fluid intelligence (reasoning), numerical proficiency, crystallized intelligence (knowledge of general notions), and so on.

These subjects are assessed by administering standardized tests to candidates with bureaucratic names such as GLUE, MMLU, ImageNet, MATH, Grade School Math 8K (GSM8K), and Graduate-Level Google-Proof Q&A (GPQA).

We can think of them as our General Certificate of Secondary Education (GCSE) tests. But there is no need to remember their names: what matters are the skills they measure, that is, the subjects: language comprehension, math, science, images, etc. The grades on the final report card are what will decide whether an AI will receive an AGI diploma: for that, it should have positive grades in all subjects.

We will follow the group of students who take the AGI diploma exams, but we will also tell the behind-the-scenes stories that students do not see: the difficult work of the evaluators, who create the exams, to make sure that they reveal the candidates' skills as objectively as possible, and also the hard work of the teachers, who prepare the candidates to do their best.

7. There Is Always One More Exam

There is a creative tension between examiners and trainers of intelligent agents: the former look for situations in which the agent fails, the latter try to fix that flaw, in a continuous cycle. This "arms race" is pushing us to the ultimate boundaries of what is possible for technology.

Have you ever wondered why the gazelle can run faster than 50 mph even though its food—the grass—cannot run away? The answer, of course, is in the daily confrontation with the cheetah, which goes even faster, and feeds on gazelles. Every day, both must pass a major test in order to survive, and as a result, both have become extremely fast.

This "arms race" (which is technically called antagonistic co-evolution) has similarities in several technological fields, for example, in the constant competition between cryptographers (who create encrypted messages) and cryptanalysts (who decipher them), where it has pushed progress in both fields to the extreme.

The same creative tension is ongoing between agent trainers and their evaluators, a competition that will not end easily: for the former, the ideal goal would be a machine that can solve any problem; for the latter, it would be a test that is unsurpassable for any machine (but not for us). It is by no means certain that these goals are attainable, but like the gazelle and the cheetah, this process

DOI: 10.1201/9781003737339-9

pushes us to explore the limits of our possibilities. As they compete, the two antagonists are together charting the ultimate boundaries of our intelligence, and of artificial intelligence, and the impassable no-man's-lands that surround them, as yet unexplored.

The AI adventure is also an exploration of human limits.

* * *

Constructing an exam is a delicate operation: it must be easy to answer if one has understood the method, and impossible to do otherwise. The question must be clear, and the answer unambiguous, so as to avoid misunderstandings at the time of correction. If the answer is obvious to everyone, the question is useless.

These were more or less all the recommendations I received from Frank, a colleague at the University of California, Davis, where my journey had led me, and where I found myself writing exam questions for the first time. The rest I learned by making mistakes, like everyone else.

It is not easy to assess either human students or machines: how do we know what we are really measuring, especially in a world of artificial agents who are very good at finding shortcuts? How do we know that the machine has not already seen the exam questions, in a world where models read virtually the entire web? Or that the machine is not one of those students who understand the subject matter but do poorly on exams?

In the end, the problem is one of validity: who guarantees that we are measuring what we intended to measure, and not something else? Often a measurement ends up becoming a definition, so that a poorly designed test often measures only the ability to pass that test. For example, in the case of human doctors passing the theoretical exam after doing a year as a resident may reveal something useful, but passing the same exam by a computer probably reveals something very different. And then, of course, there are aspects of life that cannot (and should not) be measured, and it is by no means certain that general intelligence is an exception: it might be possible to measure so many specific abilities without ever getting to the bottom of the list.

Other traits such as attitudes, values, and personality are also measured in the human mind. Would it be wrong to attempt this in an intelligent machine? Someday, perhaps something similar might be required by law: the *AI Act* in several places mentions an obligation on the part of manufacturers to conduct evaluations of their models and gives the Commission's "AI Office" the authority to conduct such evaluations. Given that legal obligations include—for example—those related to the fair treatment of citizens, it seems clear that there will have to be methods for assessing aspects that are not purely cognitive, for example, the potential presence of gender *bias*. The exams for our creations may indeed never end.

* * *

There are now dozens of *benchmarks*, which for brevity's sake, we will not describe in this book and which measure skills such as visual reasoning, speech comprehension, computer programming, and many others. These are all created according to the same principles, which are now being formalized, perhaps setting the stage for future machine psychometrics.

The first consideration when creating a test is to ensure *validity* and *reliability*, that is, that the questions are relevant to the trait you are trying to measure and that the score does not change too much if you repeat the test several times. One of the most common ways to create test batteries is to adapt already prepared tests for other purposes, as Louis Thurstone had already done. Then we try to calibrate the difficulty of the test so that it allows us to measure the difference between the *reference population*, that is, the normative group and the machines: it is this distance that we need to observe, if we are interested in the current definition of AGI.

Do we want to develop tests that are solvable only by the most qualified human experts? Does this change the definition of AGI: pass the average person or the best expert? The nature of the tests we use will shape the direction taken by this technology and ultimately the very definition of what we consider "intelligence."

Competition between trainers and evaluators is rapidly driving the technology, and both fields are evolving rapidly. I am sure that before long, there will be companies or government agencies dedicated to the constant evaluation of intelligent agents. I would not be surprised if someday there are intelligent machines that specialize in evaluating the cognitive abilities of other intelligent machines.

All of this will be essential for recognizing a hypothetical AGI, should we ever create it or just see it on the horizon, or for figuring out how far we are from that milestone. Sooner or later, this journey will need a map.

Interlude 7a: Five levels of performance (according to DeepMind).

EMERGENT Better than an unskilled human being
COMPETENT Better than 50 percent of human beings
EXPERT Better than 90 percent of human beings
VIRTUOUS Better than 99 percent of human beings
SUPERHUMAN Better than 100 percent of human beings

Interlude 7b: Five Steps to AGI (according to OpenAI).

CONVERSATIONALISTS Machines capable of conversation
REASONERS Machines capable of reasoning
AGENTS Capable of taking actions on behalf of the user and for extended periods of time
INNOVATORS Machines capable of innovating
ORGANIZATIONS Machines equivalent to an entire organization of people

8. AGI on the Horizon

Defining AGI is not a simple task, and the lack of consensus complicates how we measure progress toward it. After all, to search for something we need to be able to recognize it, and this is pushing researchers toward ever more practical definitions. What's clear is that the concept is no longer confined to science fiction: according to some scientists, the goal may now be within reach.

Today's frontier models perform competently even on novel tasks they were not trained for, crossing a threshold that previous generations of AI and supervised deep learning systems never managed. Decades from now, they will be recognized as the first true examples of AGI, just as the 1945 ENIAC is now recognized as the first true general-purpose electronic computer.

Peter Norvig is a scientist known for many things, but not for his loquacity, and so when he speaks, experts tend to listen. It does not hurt that he is the co-author of a classic university text on AI on which an entire generation of researchers has been trained. In a 2010 article, he had announced, with perfect timing, "The Unreasonable Effectiveness of Data", or the arrival of the statistical method in AI, one that relies on *machine learning* and massive amounts of data. In the fall of 2023, in another article, he announced the arrival of AGI. It had only been 15 years since the publication of the book *Artificial General*

DOI: 10.1201/9781003737339-10

Intelligence and less than eight since the creation of the OpenAI company.

Norvig's new article had the virtue of listing the properties that, according to him, already made current AI models "general," a specific and detailed list that formed his practical definition of how to recognize an AGI.

> *These models . . . are trained on hundreds of gigabytes . . . covering any topic that has been written about online. . . . [T]hey can perform a variety of tasks, including answering questions, generating stories, summarizing, . . . making decisions, doing customer support, calling out to other services to take actions, . . . operate on images and text, but some systems also process audio and video, . . . converse in dozens of languages and translate between them, even for language pairs that have no example translations in the training data . . . and learn directly from a prompt rather than from the training data.*

Other researchers have different views on what features should define an AGI, and this is part of the challenge of looking for something without knowing exactly what it is. However, a consensus is emerging: there will not be a single test for AGI, but rather a report card that will help us compare machines and people in a number of "subjects." And those "exam subjects" increasingly resemble "psychometric" dimensions, measurable by various tests.

The article continued:

> *"General intelligence" must be thought of in terms of a multidimensional scorecard, not a single yes/no proposition. Nonetheless, there is a meaningful discontinuity between narrow and general intelligence: . . . frontier language models can perform competently at pretty much any information task that can be done by humans, can be posed and answered using natural language, and has quantifiable performance.*

In the years after ChatGPT, the time for vague definitions was coming to an end: if AGI was to be transformed from a philosophical possibility to an engineering problem, it was time to be clear about what we were trying to build. The major research groups took up the challenge.

* * *

In November 2023, the company DeepMind published a study aimed at defining practically what was meant by AGI. One of the authors was Shane Legg, co-founder of the company, and the very inventor of the phrase *AGI*. The operational definition was based on two different aspects: the variety of tasks an intelligent agent was capable of performing, and the competence achieved in those tasks, compared to humans.

The first distinction was resolved in a very simple way, distinguishing only between *narrow AI* and *general AI*, that is, there were no details on how to measure different levels of generality. AlphaGo and AlexNet were listed as *narrow*, GPT, and Gemini as *general AI*. The study, however, went into the details of how to quantify levels of performance, using humans as a "reference group" to identify five different levels of intelligence: emergent, competent, expert, virtuous, and superhuman (as shown in Interlude 7a).

These levels corresponded to being, in order: better than an unskilled human being (*emergent*), better than 50 percent of humans (*competent*), better than 90 percent of humans (*expert*), better than 99 percent of humans (*virtuous*), and better than 100 percent of humans (*superhuman*). There are similar gradations in the areas of chess (master, grandmaster, etc.), facial recognition (expert, super-recognizer, etc.), and exist for autonomous cars (semi-autonomous driving, autonomous driving, etc.).

The DeepMind article proposed using this terminology for both ANI and AGI and stated that in the case of *narrow*

AI, all levels had already been reached by some specialized system, including the superhuman level. Within its own narrow domain, Siri was competent, grammar correctors were expert, AlphaGo was a virtuoso, and its heir AlphaZero was superhuman. On the AGI side, however, the article said that only the "emerging" level had been achieved, for example, by ChatGPT, while all others were considered "not yet achieved." But that was the summer of 2023, and the world moves fast.

What was missing, from that taxonomy, were details on how to measure the distance that separates an agent from the AGI finish line, that is, how to break down the journey into stages. That was taken care of by the taxonomy proposed by their rivals, OpenAI, also shown in Interlude 7.

* * *

> *OpenAI has come up with a set of five levels to track its progress toward building artificial intelligence software capable of outperforming humans.*

With these words, a few months later, in July 2024, the Bloomberg news agency described an internal OpenAI document that divided the path to their stated goal into five stages. These five levels corresponded to different levels of generality of an intelligent system, like steps leading from *narrow* to *general*.

The first level was conversationalists (machines capable of conversation) and was listed as "achieved." It was followed by reasoners (machines capable of reasoning), which were considered within reach. Reasoning in this context means proceeding from a premise to a conclusion, with explicit steps, and there was rapid progress in this direction by the end of 2024, as we will see in Chapter 11.

The other three levels to be reached were as follows: *agents* (machines capable of taking actions on behalf of the user over many days), innovators (machines capable of innovating), and finally *organizations* (the highest level, machines equivalent to an entire organization of people). The third tier is also considered very close to realization, and many agents are already in testing, such as being able to answer mail, do grocery shopping, and talk to *customer service* on the phone.[1]

Having names helps with concrete thinking, and by combining the two taxonomies, it is possible to assign each AI model to one of the 25 different categories: for example, a *competent* reasoner would complete reasoning with similar performance to the average human being; a *virtuous* conversationalist would hold conversations better than 99 percent of people. What would be the economic value of a *skilled innovator*?

* * *

By the end of 2024, while sorting through the mass of new experimental results, the mood had changed. The 2007 thought experiments on the theoretical possibility of "general intelligence" had given way to online leaderboards, in which real models compete with each other to be the first to outperform humans in rigorous examinations. In just 15 years, the tense had gone from the future of dreamers to the past of Norvig's article and other studies, all seeking to standardize terminology to understand where this journey is taking us, inform the public, and regulate the field.

In 2024, there was still no AGI because there were at least three levels missing: *agents*, *innovators*, and *organizations*. Peter Norvig was probably being optimistic: it is one thing to recognize the destination on the horizon, but another thing to reach it. The evaluators' job is to measure that gap, and the trainers' job is to close it. Assuming that AGI's goal is attainable, how far is it?

In October 2023, the organization *AI Impacts* conducted a survey of 2,778 industry experts, asking them to predict the year when autonomous machines will be able "to complete any task better and more economically than a human worker." This definition obviously goes far beyond AGI's, but the results were surprising: 10 percent of respondents expected it by 2027, and 50 percent before 2047.

Six months later, in May 2024, a group of academics including Nobel laureate Geoff Hinton published an article in the prestigious journal "Science" to point out the potential risks of this technology and take stock of the situation. Their language was not that of science fiction, but the sober language of engineering.

> *Companies are engaged in a race to create generalist AI systems that match or exceed human abilities in most cognitive work . . . . There is no fundamental reason for AI progress to slow or halt at human-level abilities. Indeed, AI has already surpassed human abilities in narrow domains such as playing strategy games and predicting how proteins fold. Compared with humans, AI systems can act faster, absorb more knowledge, and communicate at a higher bandwidth. Additionally, they can be scaled to use immense computational resources and can be replicated by the millions. We do not know for certain how the future of AI will unfold. However, we must take seriously the possibility that highly powerful generalist AI systems that outperform human abilities across many critical domains will be developed within this decade or the next.*

* * *

A few years after the first language models such as GPT, AGI was no longer a dream or a topic of science fiction: many investors were betting that the road to AGI was open. Two directions of progress were seen as promising for approaching that goal: increasing the scale of models (i.e., their size), and studying architectures capable of performing simple reasoning.

The journey continues, and those two paths will be described in the next chapters.

Interlude 8. Two different ways of thinking.

Answering these questions requires two completely different ways of thinking.

Can you notice the difference?

Question for "MODE 1": complete this scenario

Situation: A woman is cooking in the kitchen. She picks up a pot and then . . . .

Possible completions:

A) She starts to boil water.
B) She goes out to do some gardening.
C) He turns on the television.
D) He starts to play with his dog.

Answer: A | B | C | D
(Taken from HellaSWAG, common sense test)

* * *

Question for "MODE 2": *calculate the answer*
James writes a three-page letter to two different friends twice a week.
How many pages does he write a year?

Answer: [?]
Steps:
*He writes each friend 3*2=6 6 pages a week*
*So he writes 6*2=12 pages every week*
(There are 52 weeks in a year)
*That means he writes 12*52=624 pages a year*

The answer is: 624

(Taken from GSM8K, elementary math test)

note

[1] In 2026, both reasoners and agents are available.

9. Two Ways of Thinking, Two Roads Ahead

Where does the journey stand, mapless, toward a hypothetical "human-level" intelligence? At least two roads may lie ahead: one for the problems we solve at a glance, and another for those that require thinking one step at a time.

Imagine you have a deck consisting of 25 playing cards and consider two seemingly similar questions: is it possible for a single card to cover the entire screen of your television? And is it possible for all the cards to cover it?

In the first case, you can answer immediately and unconsciously; in the second case, you take longer, performing deliberate and explicit mental operations. The difference between how we answer these two questions is of great interest to psychologists, who sometimes speak of two different ways of thinking: intuition (an involuntary, implicit, fast process) and reasoning (a voluntary, explicit, slow process). Nobel laureate Daniel Kahneman called them "System 1" and "System 2," respectively, and this distinction is useful in understanding the direction research is taking.

Many researchers have begun to propose preliminary *roadmaps*, that is, lists of steps that will take us toward a form of AGI. The one proposed by OpenAI lists at the second level the ability to *reason*, and this is a technical term: it means the ability to follow a series of explicit steps leading from a premise to a conclusion. The question is

DOI: 10.1201/9781003737339-11

whether the method followed so far, of language models such as GPT, will be able to produce a form of reasoning, or whether other innovations will be necessary before the second level is conquered.

The distinction between System 1 and System 2 is not sufficient to form the report card for the examination subjects, but it does provide a useful guide to summarize the results of the many tests conducted so far: in some problems, AI has quickly achieved human-like performance, and in others, this is proving more difficult. For System 1 problems, it seems that increasing the size of data and models solves many difficulties. It is the problems of the second type, those requiring System 2, that offer the most resistance: reasoning problems.

* * *

> *The world's smartest computer scientists, it seems, have created artificial intelligence that is more liberal arts major than numbers whiz.*

With these words, in the summer of 2024, the *New York Times* reiterated what had been a concern from the start for the creators of models like GPT: many of the *benchmarks* used contained typical System 1 problems, such as recognizing sentences of similar meaning, or whether a given sentence expresses a positive or negative sentiment. Many of these problems had been solved simply by increasing the scale of the models, that is, their size. But the trick did not seem to work for typical System 2 problems.

For example, in the MMLU *benchmark* described in previous chapters, the GPT 3.5 model scored above the 90th percentile in disciplines such as history, psychology, and politics, but below the 40th percentile in subjects such as physics, statistics, and chemistry.

Predictably, evaluators had smelled the weakness and immediately set about creating batteries of tests specifically to measure reasoning skills. As before, the names of the tests are unpronounceable acronyms, but do not worry: what matters is what they measure. The basic ones are devoted to elementary math (the test is called GSM8K, from the initials of *Grade School Math, 8000 questions*), advanced math (the test is called MATH), and scientific reasoning (the test is called GPQA, or Google-Proof *Question Answers*, and contains questions on scientific topics that are "Google-proof," meaning that the answer cannot be found online but must be obtained by reasoning).

We can simply call them tests of "elementary math," "advanced math," and "science," and will describe in detail only the first of the three, just to give an idea of how math reasoning skills are assessed.

System 2

How is the ability to "reason mathematically" measured? This is not the ability to compute, but to solve a complex problem by decomposing it into simple steps, as can be seen from the steps in the second question in Interlude 8. In 2021, a group of OpenAI researchers led by Karl Cobbe decided that it was time to quantify this capability, because even then they considered it the weak point of "language models" such as GPT:

> *In recent years, large language models have demonstrated impressive skills across many diverse tasks . . . . However, even the largest models falter when required to perform multi-step mathematical reasoning . . . . Mathematical reasoning thus reveals a critical weakness in modern language models.*

So they created a test of 8,500 math problems, specially written, solved, and checked by human experts, which require many steps to solve, and which are solvable by elementary and middle school students (they called it GSM8K). The questions in that test require between two and eight steps to solve, with solutions requiring performing a sequence of elementary calculations using the four arithmetic operations. The score is given by the percentage of correct answers, and guessing does not go far from zero, while human experts hover around 98 percent. At the time of its creation, traditional methods such as GPT did not exceed 50 percent.

These were the problems that worried model trainers and intrigued evaluators because they revealed a specific weakness in a method that was otherwise performing great in intuition-like problems.

System 1

For comparison, consider an "intuition" problem, that is, one in which the correct answer is recognized "at a glance." The economist Herbert Simon had defined intuition as "nothing more and nothing less than a form of recognition": this is how we recognize—for example—a dog from a fox, even before we list in words the physical characteristics that distinguish them.

As an example, I briefly describe below a single test in this category, used to assess what is called "common sense" and which is very useful in the creation of agents who must interact with people. As before, the name of the test is ugly, but we will not need to remember it: it is called HellaSWAG, and it was created in 2018 by Yejin Choi of the University of Washington. It consists of 100,000 questions like this one, where we have to find the most plausible completion of a scene:

> *On stage, a woman takes a seat at the piano. She a) sits on a bench as her sister plays with the doll. b) smiles with someone as the music plays. c) is in the crowd, watching the dancers. d) nervously sets her fingers on the keys.*

People get a score of 95.6 percent. At the time of its creation, GPT answered 50 percent of the questions correctly, but in 2020, it jumped to 85 percent and the following year to 95.3 percent. Once again, within a few years, a *benchmark* explicitly designed to be unconquerable by an AI had been solved, simply by increasing the size of the model. Problems whose answer is recognized "at a glance" are conquered by increasing model scale, while those whose answer requires "thinking one step at a time," that is, reasoning, seem to require other innovations.

* * *

We are engaged in a mapless journey to a destination that may not exist: how do we know if we are on the right track? This may be generally true for everyone, but at least in the search for a hypothetical AGI, we now have two promising avenues to explore: the scaling hypothesis and that of reasoning to emulate Systems 1 and 2. They may not be enough, but we have to start somewhere, so in the next two chapters, we will describe both.

Interlude 9. Differences in scale.

What can we do with 1 euro, with 1,000 euros, and with 1,000,000 euros? We can buy a coffee, a smartphone, or a villa with a pool. At each step, we are changing order of magnitude (three orders, in this case), an increase that is called an exponential in mathematics. With 1,000,000,000 euros, we can build London's Wembley Stadium.

The same reality at different orders of magnitude has different behaviors in economics as in physics. It is useful to get used to thinking in terms of orders of magnitude and their names in a world that grows exponentially. We all know the difference between meters and kilometers, but the same language can be applied to other quantities: coffee costs a euro, a smartphone a kilo-euro, and a mansion a mega-euro. Wembley Stadium costs a giga-euro.

The size of a file? We can approximate: a word, a maximum of ten bytes; a text message on WhatsApp, a kilobyte; attach to it a photo in high definition, a megabyte; download a song in mp3 format, five megabytes; download a movie in full high definition, a gigabyte; and saving a collection of 300 movies can reach terabytes.

The tools, administrative and cultural, needed to manage an organization of people are different at different scales: a house may have as few as a couple of inhabitants, a country may contain a kilo-inhabitant, a nation a mega-inhabitant, and a continent a giga-inhabitant.

The size of AI systems is rapidly changing by orders of magnitude, and this change in scale is the key to their success. But the cultural and technical tools to understand them are struggling to follow because they have been developed at different levels.

The LeNet neural network in the 1990s had about 60,000 parameters; AlexNet in 2012 had about 60 million parameters; GPT 2 had about 1 billion parameters; and GPT 4 had about 1 trillion. These sizes not only require different infrastructure and expertise but also give rise to different phenomena.

10. The Scaling Hypothesis

Some cognitive properties of AI models emerge only at a certain scale, that is, when their size exceeds a certain order of magnitude. Some researchers speculate that this effect will continue to improve the performance of the present technology. This conjecture is known as the "scaling hypothesis" and it follows from it that the way forward is to increase computational and data resources. Others, however, think that further innovations will be needed before a form of AGI is achieved.

> *Model performance depends most strongly on scale, which consists of three factors: the number of model parameters N, the size of the dataset D, and the amount of compute C used for training. . . . Our results strongly suggest that larger models will continue to perform better.*

With these words, in January 2020, one of the first experimental studies of language models formulated the conjecture that models of larger scale would perform better. The authors were all OpenAI researchers. A few months later, a blog post by Gwern Branwen gave this idea a suggestive name that we still use today: *The Scaling Hypothesis*. Since then, that name has been in scientific articles, in investor reports, and probably on the desk of many politicians.

So far, the facts seem to prove those researchers right: in 2019, GPT-2 was scoring 32.4 percent on "language comprehension" tests (MMLU tests), well below the

DOI: 10.1201/9781003737339-12

human level, while in 2022, GPT-4 was scoring 88.7 percent, a level comparable to the human level. The main difference between the two was scale: the former had 1 billion parameters, trained using 40 billion *tokens* (i.e., words or parts of words); the latter had 1 trillion parameters, trained (it seems) using 10 trillion tokens. A growth of three orders of magnitude, achieved in three years, had brought the model to the threshold of human performance.

The idea of course was not new: already AlexNet in 2012 had learned to recognize the images of thousands of objects, using the same architecture that LeNet had used in 1997 to recognize the numbers 0 to 9, handwritten. But it had used 60 million, instead of 60,000, parameters: three orders of magnitude more.

This effect is one of the main drivers of progress in the field of AI, and it explains the rush by companies to acquire more data, more hardware, and more power to train bigger and bigger models. And in recent years, this trend has been accelerating: according to a study by Epoch AI (a San Francisco-based research institute), since AlexNet, the amount of data used to train leading models in AI has increased about 2.9 times each year, and the amount of computation needed for training has grown 4.1 times per year (about an order of magnitude every 2 to 3 years). Since parameter growth has changed pace, performance has rapidly increased on many *benchmarks*, as we have seen in previous chapters.

* * *

The scaling hypothesis is not new: the classic article *The Bitter Lesson* by Richard Sutton, a pioneer in *machine learning*, in 2019 began:

> *The biggest lesson that can be read from 70 years of AI research is that general methods that leverage computation are ultimately the most effective, and by a large margin. The ultimate reason for this is Moore's law, or rather its generalization of continued exponentially falling cost per unit of computation.*

In other words, the performance of an intelligent agent grows as its scale increases, and this relationship can be described mathematically, through formulas called scaling *laws*. Some abilities emerge only after certain sizes have been reached. Many researchers think this can continue, and so they propose to "climb" to larger and larger orders of magnitude, in the hope of creating models that are not only more accurate but also more general.

This is the most important question in the field of AI and in the minds of managers and investors: can a form of AGI be achieved simply by continuing to scale up models, or are there skills that will require entirely new discoveries and ideas? In the former case, one must invest in more resources, and in the latter, in more research, if we are to complete the journey.

* * *

Right now, the industry is betting that scaling up can solve at least the problems we called "System 1" in the previous chapter, that is, those that do not require explicit reasoning, and many of these have great economic value. Separately, there is a serious scientific debate about how to conquer problems that require reasoning, and we will discuss this in the next chapter. As for problems of the first kind, one question to ask is: What factors can limit the creation of ever-larger models? Much will depend on three resources: data, hardware, and energy.

The Data Wall

One of the laws of *machine learning* is that to train bigger models, you need more data. And if we intend to scale models by many orders of magnitude, the amount of data will have to follow accordingly. How many orders of magnitude are still available, in terms of data? At what point will the usable data run out, and what can be done at that point? In June 2024, a study by Epoch AI compared the growth rate of data available online and that of data required to train AI. The conclusion was that the consumption of data is growing faster than its production: "Our results indicate that if current trends in language model development continue, models will be trained on data roughly equal in size to the entire available stock of human text between 2026 and 2032."

The "Compute" Wall

Moore's Law is the observation that in the history of computers, computational power doubles every 18 months (technically, the number of operations per second for the same cost), and so in just over five years, a whole order of magnitude is crossed. But the amount of operations required to train a model is increasing by an order of magnitude every two years; that is, demand will become greater than supply. GPT 3.5 used 2.6 billion petaFLOPs in 2022, Llama 3 used 38 billion petaFLOPs in 2024 (a FLOP is the name given in computer science to an elementary operation, and it stands for: *Floating Point Operation*; a petaFLOP consists of 10^{15} such operations).

The Energy Wall

More computation requires more energy. In today's data centers, there are thousands of H100 chips from Nvidia Corp., each drawing 700 watts or 7 old incandescent light bulbs. And then there are the cooling costs. Epoch AI estimated that training GPT 3 cost $4 million, while training GPT 4 cost $40 million. The environmental impact and economic cost of this technology deserve serious consideration.

* * *

The *Scaling Hypothesis* takes artificial intelligence into superhuman territory not only in terms of performance but also in terms of resources. It is already becoming normal to build a new computing center specifically to train a new AI model, and there is even talk of starting to create power plants specifically to power a computing center. Every publishing house has been approached by computer companies to buy catalog and archive rights. How much energy, data, and computation does it make sense to spend on creating an AI? The answer depends on the value of the information it will be able to provide: what are we creating?

"You can't connect the dots looking forward; you can only connect them looking backwards": this is how Steve Jobs described his observation to Stanford undergraduates that the meaning of a journey is only understood at the end. Today, I wonder if the new AI, capable of distilling millions of books, could make sense of a phenomenon I have been wondering about for some time. How many books do we write that have only a handful of readers: autobiographies, essays, manuals, invectives, and fictional stories. For each, there are hundreds of hours of work by editors, writers, typesetters, and graphic designers: facts are double-checked, prose cleaned up, and bibliographic references checked. And then, there are the dissertations that almost no one reads, except students and professors, and the obscure journal articles that certainly no one reads, except authors and editors.

Why do we do this?

Sometimes, I imagine how our great-grandchildren will view this moment in history. Perhaps it will make sense looking at it from the future: perhaps they will say that we were forming an immense artificial mind, and every extra page provided a drop of knowledge.

Interlude 10. Reasoning test.

QUESTION:

"John has three apples. He buys four more and then gives two to his friend. How many apples does John have now?"

From: GSM8K Battery (elementary math)

* * *

QUESTION:

"Samantha ran 5 miles a day for 3 days. Then she ran two more miles on the fourth day. How many miles did Samantha run in total?"

From: GSM8K Battery (elementary math)

* * *

QUESTION:

A reaction of a liquid organic compound, whose molecules consist of carbon and hydrogen atoms, is performed at 80 centigrade and 20 bar for 24 hours.

In the proton nuclear magnetic resonance spectrum, the signals with the highest chemical shift of the reactant are replaced by a signal of the product that is observed about three to four units downfield.

Compounds from which position in the periodic system of the elements, which are also used in the corresponding large-scale industrial process, have mostly likely initially been added in small amounts?

A) A metal compound from the fifth period.
B) A metal compound from the fifth period and a non-metal compound from the third period.
C) A metal compound from the fourth period.
D) A metal compound from the fourth period and a non-metal compound from the second period

From: Chemistry in GPQA (advanced science questions)

11. Reasoning One Step at a Time

Can today's language models be induced to reason "one step at a time" to solve reasoning problems as well? This question may hold the key to an early form of AGI, and many researchers are looking for the answer. Another competition with evaluators is in sight.

Nothing in the training and use of LLMs would seem to suggest remotely that they can do any type of principled reasoning.

In March 2024, the Annals of the New York Academy of Sciences published these words in an article by Subbarao Kambhampati, a professor at Arizona State University. The title posed a direct question, "Can large language models reason and plan?", and the last paragraph gave an answer, "To summarize, nothing that I have read, verified, or done gives me any compelling reason to believe that LLMs do reasoning/planning, as normally understood."

The timing could not have been more delicate: companies officially dedicated to pursuing an early form of AGI had to convince investors that they were capable of completing that journey. Among them was, of course, OpenAI, which was to raise funds that summer and had publicly identified *reasoning* as the second stage to be reached: that referred to the ability to proceed from a premise to a conclusion by a series of explicit steps, that is, the way of thinking described as "System 2" in Chapter 9.

DOI: 10.1201/9781003737339-13

Kambhampati spent the summer of 2024 repeating his skeptic message at a series of international AI conferences, sometimes with a dismissive tone toward those who expect a neural network to actually be able to "reason." How could he be so sure? The professor was specialized in an area far removed from neural networks and language models: planning algorithms, a classic discipline of what is often called "good old fashioned AI", that is closely related to formal reasoning methods.

A planning problem requires determining a sequence of actions leading from an initial state to an end state, the goal. The classic example is the problem of solving a Rubik's cube by finding a sequence of moves that transform the shuffled cube into the solved cube. What makes the problem difficult is considering the consequences of a move, which could lead the state of the cube further away from the goal: planning requires a form of foresight, and this is not part of the "intuitive" thinking typical of neural networks. On the contrary, intuition in these cases can be misleading. Something had to be modified.

Kambhampati had therefore taken on the role of "evaluator," creating a test designed to measure this specific ability; he had called it PlanBench; a typical question was as follows:

A PlanBench Problem

I am playing with a set of blocks where I need to arrange the blocks into stacks. Here are the actions I can do: Pick up a block, Unstack a block from on top of another block, Put down a block, Stack a block on top of another block.

As initial conditions, I have that: the red block is clear, the blue block is clear, the yellow block is clear, the hand is empty, the blue block is on top of the orange block, the red block is on the table, the orange block is on the table and the yellow block is on the table.

My goal is to have the orange block on top of the blue block.

The solution to this type of question is a sequence of "valid" actions that transforms the starting situation into the desired one: that is, a "plan." Purely mathematical algorithms have existed for decades that can solve these problems when posed in a strict mathematical format, but the important question is whether a model such as GPT can reason and plan so that it can be used while considering problems expressed in natural language or even in visual form. This ability (or the lack thereof) is probably why the "scientific" components of benchmarks like MMLU resist the benefits of the *Scaling Hypothesis*.

Kambhampati's conclusion was that GPT-4 solved only a small percentage of PlanBench questions correctly, and thus—in his view—was incapable of reasoning. His voice joined that of other researchers, including Emily Bender who had called the language models "parrots," capable only of repeating things they had already seen, without really understanding them. The issue needed to be resolved, not only because a parrot is not endowed with "human-level" intelligence but also because this ability was exactly what OpenAI had publicly listed as "the second level" in the climb toward AGI, and investors were watching them.

For both classical AI researchers and new AI companies, the stakes were high: for the former, symbolic reasoning was the last frontier yet unviolated by the language model revolution; for the latter, there was a credibility problem with their plan to achieve a form of AGI. Having conquered most linguistic tasks, by the summer of 2024, the question of reasoning had become urgent.

Thinking One Step at a Time

There is an idea that could solve the problem, and it stems from an observation made in 2022 by Jason Wei: if GPT is asked to think aloud, describing the steps one at a time, it makes fewer mistakes in reasoning tasks. The curious method was called the "chain of thought" and diligently reported at the NeurIPS conference saying, "generating a chain of thought—a series of intermediate reasoning steps—significantly improves the ability of large language models to perform complex reasoning."

Before discussing how this strange effect can be exploited, let us observe it in action.

> QUESTION: The cafeteria had 23 apples. If they used 20 to make lunch and bought 6 more, how many apples do they have?
>
> Model output without explicit reasoning.
> ANSWER: The answer is 27.
>
> Model Output with explicit reasoning:
>
> STEPS: The cafeteria had 23 apples originally.
> They used 20 to make lunch.
> So they had 23 – 20 = 3.
> They bought 6 more apples, so they have 3 + 6 = 9.
> ANSWER: The answer is 9

In short, just as it is useful for humans to have a piece of paper on which to scribble intermediate results while thinking about a problem, in AI models, this function is performed by describing all the steps "aloud." The next move was natural: instead of exploiting this spontaneous ability of the models, why not refine it with specific examples of useful and valid reasoning chains, technically called "rationales"?

This became a secret project within OpenAI and other research groups. Rumors circulated during the summer of 2024 of a mysterious "strawberry project," and at one point, the company's CEO, Sam Altman, posted a picture of strawberries on social media. Then one day, an X/Twitter profile that seemed very familiar with OpenAI's internal affairs wrote "Welcome to level two," showing the strawberry icon.

The allusion to the five levels of AGI was clear.

* * *

With great timing, just a few weeks after the end of Subbarao Kambhampati's summer tour exhibiting the poor results of GPT and the like on PlanBench and some other reasoning benchmarks, on September 12, 2024, the OpenAI company announced the news it had jealously guarded for months, publishing an article with a title that said it all: *Learning to reason with large language models*.

The article introduced for the first time "o1," the new model mentioned in Chapter 6. Remember the one that "joined the class" in the fall of 2024? Although it was officially called "o1," everyone simply called it *strawberry*. The technical details remained secret, but the basic idea was explained: "o1" had an inner monologue, which it could control and make plausible, if not correct. The whole process was slow, just as in the case of System 2, but it worked: the new algorithm outperformed their previous model, GPT-4o, on 54 of the 57 MMLU categories, and the main gains were observed precisely in the science categories. On the whole MMLU benchmark, it had thus reached 92.3 percent, surpassing humans, who stopped at 89.8 percent.

But that was not all: "o1" was also scoring high on "competitive programming" tests (a kind of Olympic discipline among programmers), achieving gold-medal-level scores, beating more than 90 percent of human programmers. In the elementary and advanced mathematics examinations, it reached or exceeded the scores of humans (so that the two *benchmarks* GSM8K and MATH were declared "saturated" and set aside). The same had also happened with the advanced science test (GPQA). So, the researchers had created a new, even more difficult test, consisting of math exams aimed at the best American high school students. They scored among the nation's top 500 students and above the threshold for admission to the American Mathematical Olympiad.

As evaluators rushed to study new tests for this model, by fall 2024, investors' doubts had been assuaged, and a few weeks later, OpenAI completed a new round of funding.

* * *

What about professor Kambhampati, who had spent the summer of 2024 predicting that neural networks would be unable to reason because they perform too poorly on PlanBench?

A few weeks later, he co-published a report showing that "o1" had reached 97.8 percent on PlanBench, up from 34 percent of GPT-4, but he pointed out that performance worsened when asked to make plans that included a large number of objects and many steps. Humans achieve about 78% on the same version of the benchmark, while specialized algorithms can achieve 100%.

The original PlanBench task is now almost saturated: various reasoning models (including OpenAI's o1 and DeepSeek's R1, an open-source model that arrived in January 2025) now score around 98 percent on standard Blocksworld. But harder variants of the test have been proposed. One of them replaces words like block and stack with random words, like feast and apple, to prevent the model from using common-sense "intuition" about the physical world. Here, the best performance of reasoning models declines to around 50 percent, above that of standard LLMs, but lower than what can be achieved with bespoke mathematical methods.

Whatever its theoretical limits, this level of reasoning has proved sufficient for the tasks that matter most in practical benchmarks: these same models now perform near the level of the best human experts in competitive programming, advanced mathematics, and physics. It turns out that many scientific questions probably do not depend on very deep and exact planning.

In the summer of 2025, a specialized descendant of o1, an experimental model OpenAI called its "IMO model", participated in the International Mathematical Olympiad and achieved a gold-medal score, placing in the top 12 percent of all participants.

The debate still goes on, another example of the natural skepticism of all scientists, and of our very human reluctance to admit defeat.

"Yes, but . . . ."

Interlude 11. The comet.

The first time I trained a neural network, it had at most a dozen synaptic weights, and it took a few minutes to learn how to recognize the risk of diabetes, from about 700 examples. It was just an exercise for a master's exam in London.

I should have marked the date because it was the first of a long series, but I could reconstruct it because I remember that night when I came out of the lab, there was a comet in the starry sky over my beloved Royal Holloway, University of London, and I took that as a good sign for the future. I also remember that in those days, I had just been offered the chance to do a PhD in Bristol, and I did not know whether to accept: my initial plan was to return home after my master's degree, and I did not know what I would find in Bristol.

But there is always time to stop, and that little victory with the neural network had given me some courage, and the comet had done the rest, so that night I decided to continue the journey, at least for a while.

III.

Artificial Super Intelligence: ASI

Artificial Super Intelligence (ASI): a hypothetical form of Artificial Intelligence that would surpass human intelligence in every cognitive aspect, including creativity, problem solving and general knowledge; or perform cognitive tasks that are beyond human abilities.

There is no reason why the technology we are developing should be limited to performing "human-level tasks." In this third part, we consider the space to be explored among the tasks that are not accessible to humans, or the levels of performance that we cannot achieve: that is, the territory of superhuman AI. The question of how to share the world with machines that are smarter than us should at least be considered.

12. Reluctance and Vertigo

The closer we get to building intelligent machines, the more reluctant we seem to admit that this can be possible. We have been moving the goalposts since Alan Turing's time.

> *I grant you that you can make machines do all the things you have mentioned but you will never be able to make one to do X.*

These words appear in the famous 1950 article that gave rise to AI research, where Alan Turing devotes a section to the most common objections to the idea of an intelligent machine. One of these is what he calls the "Arguments from various disabilities," namely, the idea that there are some things that the machine can never do and for some reason would be indispensable to intelligence. He then continues:

> *Numerous features X are suggested in this connection I offer a selection: Be kind, resourceful, beautiful, friendly, have initiative, have a sense of humour, tell right from wrong, make mistakes, fall in love, enjoy strawberries and cream, make someone fall in love with it, learn from experience, use words properly, be the subject of its own thought, have as much diversity of behaviour as a man, do something really new. No support is usually offered for these statements.*

DOI: 10.1201/9781003737339-15

Was this reluctance the first sign of today's competition between trainers and evaluators of intelligent machines? Many of the skills listed earlier can be measured and then turned into a test: learning from experience, using words appropriately, and doing something really new. Others involve a presumed emotional life of the machine (not the user) and thus would be unobservable in principle.

Understanding of language? Passed. General culture? Passed. Elementary mathematics? Passed. Science, advanced math, image recognition? All passed, sometimes with scores higher than human scores. If we had seen this technology ten years ago, we would have been dumbfounded, yet when confronted with these results, even today our response is often the same one described by Alan Turing in 1950: "I grant you that, but . . . ."

* * *

A very similar list appeared 73 years later in the article in which Peter Norvig argues that an early form of AGI already exists. The second part of that article addresses the phenomenon of our stubborn reluctance to accept this idea.

> *Frontier models have achieved a significant level of general intelligence, according to the everyday meanings of those two words. And yet most commenters have been reluctant to say so for, it seems to us, four main reasons.*

Below is how Norvig lists some of the possible causes:

> *A healthy skepticism about metrics for AGI; an ideological commitment to alternative AI theories or techniques; a devotion to human (or biological) exceptionalism; a concern about the economic implications of AGI.*

The most useful and concrete objection is skepticism toward the use of metrics to measure intelligence, and it relates to the problem of the "validity" of psychometric tests: how do we know that a given measurement truly reflects the trait we intend to measure? This objection merits study from different disciplines: for example, it is obvious that answering all the questions correctly in a law or medical school exam does not necessarily mean that one can practice law or medicine. Similarly, language proficiency should not be confused with intelligence, just because often (but not always) in people, these two aspects are related. Here, we are evaluating intelligent systems that are completely different from us, where these correlations should not be taken for granted.

The other objections in Norvig's list are more ideological: that only a human or biological or logic-based being deserves the title of intelligent is not a claim that can be evaluated experimentally. Instead, our reluctance, which is its source, deserves serious consideration.

* * *

We are a strange and fascinating species: while we spend billions trying to build a machine that can think, at the same time, we refuse to accept that this is possible. We seek and together fear that encounter.

In a few years, the dream of creating an intelligence capable of competing with us has turned into a concrete project, and today, we have an open road ahead of us and the means to travel it. By increasing the scale of our creations, carefully choosing the data with which to instruct them, and modifying their architecture to help them reason and think, it is possible that in a few years they will be close to the finish line. With every single test, we see them getting closer, and so we rush to create another test, the result of which seems more reassuring. The road beckons and frightens us, promising adventure and opportunities, but also danger and failure.

I know well that feeling at the sight of the open road, the anxiety, the exhilaration, and the trepidation. It takes me back to the beginnings of my journey and the choice to accept the challenge: to me, it has always felt like vertigo, the same as one feels when faced with an abyss. This mixture of longing and reluctance is probably what early humans felt every time before venturing into new territory, when something mysterious called them to enter an uncharted world.

We should not be afraid of the anxiety that grips us before we face the unknown; perhaps, this is the moment when we are most human.

Interlude 12. The AI report card in 2024 (The grade is expressed as a percentage of the human grade).

Subject	Examination	Rated
Reading and writing skills (literacy skills) And crystallized intelligence (ability to use acquired knowledge and skills)	MMLU	102%
Visual processing (ability to perceive and manipulate visual patterns)	ImageNet	103%
Fluid intelligence (quantitative capabilities)	MATH	105%
Fluid intelligence (quantitative capabilities)	GSM8K	99%
Fluent, domain-specific knowledge (specialized knowledge in particular fields)	GPQA	107%
Common Sense	HellaSWAG	100.5%

***Note:* In 2026**, the AI/human performance ratio is 104% on ImageNet; 103% on MMLU (GPT-5.5); 107% on MATH (o3); 104% on GSM8K (fully saturated); 127% on GPQA Diamond (Gemini 3.1 Pro); and 101% on HellaSwag (Claude 3 Opus class, benchmark now retired).

13. The Final Challenge: Artificial Super Intelligence?

If AGI means machines equaling us at the tasks that define us, can we imagine a step beyond? This could take two forms: surpassing us at those same tasks, or performing tasks we cannot even conceive of. These are the two faces of a hypothetical superintelligence (ASI, Artificial Super Intelligence) and the possibility is being seriously debated in both academic and industrial circles.

If we were to reach a form of AGI, I do not think that would be the end of the journey: the traveler does not really decide the destination.

In October 2024, the Nobel Prize in physics was awarded to Geoff Hinton, co-inventor of the backpropagation algorithm, as well as AlexNet. In the press conference that followed the announcement, the British professor said of AI,

> *It will be comparable with the Industrial Revolution. But instead of exceeding people in physical strength, it's going to exceed people in intellectual ability. . . . We have no experience of what it's like to have things smarter than us.*

Hinton was not trying to impress, but to express a thought that had been bothering him for some time, and not just him. Ilya Sutskever, his former student and co-creator of GPT, had chosen these words in June of that year to return to the public after leaving OpenAI: "Superintelligence is

DOI: 10.1201/9781003737339-16

within reach. Building safe superintelligence is the most important technical problem of our time."

The two scientists were referring to the concept of ASI, which is now being seriously discussed in academic, industrial, and political circles: a form of AI that goes beyond that of humans. How did we come to seriously consider this topic, which might seem like science fiction, in universities around the world?

The competition between trainers and evaluators of intelligent agents has long been pushing AI into intellectual regions that are increasingly forbidding to humans, and so scientists are contemplating the theoretical possibility that there might be an overtake, followed by a widening gap. The four models we have been following throughout this book (Claude, Llama, GPT, and Gemini) are becoming ever more intelligent.

The idea itself is not new: as early as 1950, Alan Turing said: ". . . it seems probable that once the machine thinking method had started, it would not take long to outstrip our feeble powers." And his former collaborator I.J. Good in 1965 had devoted an entire essay to this concept, entitled *Speculations concerning the first ultra-intelligent machine*, in which he first gave the definition still in vogue today: "Let an ultraintelligent machine be defined as a machine that can far surpass all the intellectual activities of any man, however clever."

A technology that can match humans in cognitive tasks typical to us could probably also surpass them. As for the time required, robotics pioneer Hans Moravec noted in a famous 1988 essay, "After the initial successes our culture was able to far surpass biological flight in a few decades."

But the idea of overtaking is probably misleading because it pushes us to think of performance superior to our own, in the same tasks that are typical of humans. This obviously misses the real target: the possibility that a machine can perform tasks, or understand things, that we cannot even contemplate.

Imagine if a civilization of squirrels defined a form of super-intelligent AI by requiring it to do all their tasks better than they do. This technology would perhaps help them gather more nuts, but it would never discover chemistry or computer science, or other potentially valuable knowledge. Why not imagine cognitive problems that are completely foreign to human nature? There is no physical or mathematical law against this, since we do not have "universal" intelligence and are indeed very specialized. The only reason this seems impossible is our innate reluctance to accept this thought.

While we consider an AI that can beat us at our own game, therefore, let us also consider an AI that is capable of engaging in entirely different games, that is, of understanding things that our minds might be incapable of comprehending, just as the squirrel mind is incapable of learning Latin declensions or mathematical models of the atmosphere (or imagining that they might exist).

Of course, the reverse is also true: there may be things that we do easily that will always be off-limits to machines: why not? We will soon discover them because the competition between AI trainers and evaluators is rapidly leading us to explore those very boundaries.

Let us therefore consider, at least as a possibility, the idea of "super-intelligent" machines. Researcher and entrepreneur Ray Kurzweil, who now works for Google, has been arguing for more than two decades that this time will come in 2029. It is also prudent to consider as of now what might happen after an initial overtaking, that is, a possible intelligence gap.

Interlude 13. A Flynn effect for machines?

A person's intelligence cannot be reduced to a single value, but in some cases, it is still summarized with a number called the intelligence quotient (IQ). This is calculated to have a mean of 100 and a standard deviation of 15, in a reference population.

In the mid-1980s, James Flynn, a philosophy professor working in New Zealand, set out to compare scores on various IQ tests conducted in different countries and in different years.

His aim was to study the effects of cultural differences on these results.

Instead, he made a far more surprising discovery: there was a clear and gradual rise in scores, about three points per decade, throughout the century, regardless of location. This is a consistent effect, comparable to almost two standard deviations over a century, which Flynn later summarized in these words, "We get far more questions right on I.Q. tests than each succeeding generation back to the time that they were invented. Indeed, if you score the people a century ago against modern norms, they would have an average I.Q. of 70. If you score us against their norms, we would have an average I.Q. of 130."

Since then, similar results have been observed by many researchers in countries as diverse as Denmark, Spain, and Norway. The explanation is not known but seems related to progress in education. The steady increase in IQ over the years today is called the *Flynn effect*.

Can we expect a similar effect in intelligent machines, and imagine a future populated by increasingly capable ones?

14. Beating Us at Our Own Game

Beating us at our own game would be the most obvious form of superhuman intelligence, just by not stopping after reaching AGI. The implications would be profound for society, creating competition for large numbers of workers.

Consider this news story, which appeared on April 29, 1962, in the *New York Times*.

> *Not all the philosophers of the computer business admit that computers can really think. . . . In spite of many loose statements to the contrary, no existing computer can translate a foreign language as well as a bright high-school student. Other simple human tasks, such as writing rudimentary TV scripts, they cannot do at all.*

Compare it with these two other news stories, both of which appeared in the summer of 2023. The first is from Brussels and appeared in *Politico*.

> *The EU's translation unit is doubling down on artificial intelligence. For the first time, high-tech machines will translate press releases without any human oversight, in order to cut waiting time for journalists and expand the number of languages available to the public.*

The second comes from Hollywood and was featured in the *New York Times*.

DOI: 10.1201/9781003737339-17

The tentative deal announced this week by the Writers Guild of America . . . sets a monumental precedent for labor relations in a digital future. . . . The parties agreed that A.I. is not a writer. The studios cannot use A.I. in place of a credited and paid guild member. Studios can rely on A.I. to generate a first draft, but the writers to whom they deliver it get the credit.

Let us ask ourselves: is it really so unthinkable that the AI can beat us at our own game? That after an initial overtaking, there would be a gap? Let us examine a few different areas.

* * *

Dario Amodei is the founder of Anthropic, the company that created Claude, and he does not like the term "AGI," so he prefers to call the same goal "powerful AI." In an essay published in 2024, Amodei talks about the future he expects in a few years, perhaps even by 2026, and describes the kind of AI he expects this way:

In terms of pure intelligence it is smarter than a Nobel Prize winner across most relevant fields—biology, programming, math, engineering, writing, etc. . . . It can be given tasks that take hours, days, or weeks to complete, and then goes off and does those tasks autonomously, in the way a smart employee would, asking for clarification as necessary.

He then explains that it is possible to create millions of identical copies of the same entity in a huge data center, adding:

Each of these million copies can act independently on unrelated tasks, or if needed can all work together in the same way humans would collaborate, perhaps with different subpopulations fine-tuned to be especially good at particular tasks. We could summarize this as a "country of geniuses in a datacenter."

This is one of the extreme positions heard more in industry than in academia, but even the most cautious academics consider the effects of such a hypothetical technology on areas such as work and science.

Work

What could a hypothetical AGI agent do, if it were capable of performing the same cognitive tasks as humans? Probably, this agent would be able to do any job that can be done in smart working today: if there is a way to consult a doctor, a lawyer, and a teacher via chat or email, and if AI can generate the same answers, why not? Computer programming is an obvious candidate.

Of course, this would exclude what cannot be done in smart working, such as a dental hygienist, a barber, or a tire shop. What about jobs that require emotional intelligence, such as teaching? Here, a distinction must be made between the ability to feel emotions, which certainly does not belong to machines, and the ability to understand the user's emotional state, which, on the other hand, would not be at all impossible.

Science

Is it possible for an intelligent machine to produce scientific results of value to us? I do not see why not. The 2024 Nobel Prize in chemistry was awarded to two human beings for their AlphaFold algorithm results. Someday, we may see increasingly autonomous agents tasked with reading the vast scientific literature, comparing the results of similar experiments, perhaps even planning and executing new experiments. An agent equal to those existing now can already read many more books than we can read in our entire lifetimes and will soon be able to identify contradictions or surprising connections. I see no reason why these reading tasks cannot be automated, and this applies to writing and publishing tasks as well, although the readers of the future will probably not necessarily be humans. It might not be long before such an agent would take itself into territories where we could not follow.

Agents and Organizations

The last levels of the OpenAI taxonomy, the steps toward full AGI, are agents, innovators, and organizations. These are not very different from the vision described by Dario Amodei. The former should be able to receive a task and work on it for long periods of time independently. They could formulate a plan, gather the necessary information, and then execute it: organize a vacation or a business conference. Innovators might connect known information in different ways or, in principle, innovate simply because they are able to digest more information than we can, for example, by reading a million books and connecting their contents. Organizations could be comparable to a company: an entire law firm or accounting firm, for example, simulated by a group of AGIs working together to solve professional problems. But this could also be a research or artistic group, for example, intent on producing the script and images for a new film. This is possible.

* * *

When an AI is able to match people in cognitive tasks, it is not hard to imagine how it could become superhuman: the transition from AGI to ASI would happen simply by speeding up computations, increasing memory, and reducing costs. That is, waiting a few years for Moore's Law to run its course. In other words, beating us at our own game might be a direct consequence of AGI, but this would not be the most extreme form of super intelligence.

Do you dare to ask what the most extreme form is?

Interlude 14. Our Limits.

Our minds evolved by natural selection to solve problems that were life-and-death matters to our ancestors, not to commune with correctness or to answer any question we are capable of asking. We cannot hold ten thousand words in short-term memory. We cannot see in ultraviolet light. We cannot mentally rotate an object in the fourth dimension. . . . We can well imagine creatures with fewer cognitive faculties than we have . . . So why should there not be creatures with more cognitive faculties than we have, or with different ones?

(Steven Pinker, ***How the Mind Works***, 1997, p. 562)

15. Beyond the Limits of Our Intelligence

Are there things in the world that we cannot understand? I don't mean things that are incomprehensible in themselves, but incomprehensible to us humans, just as quantum mechanics is to my cat. Each mind reflects the environment in which it evolved, and this is both an advantage and a limitation.

Imagine having to compare various tools designed to filter email, as if they were candidates in a job interview. These agents observe your morning routine, analyze which emails you discard and which you keep, and the next day have to make predictions about which messages you will choose to read. The best candidate will be hired.

The simplest agent might only be able to interpret your behavior in terms of keywords and thus would have no choice but to look for the words that signal when you delete a message. Another agent might be able to formulate abstract rules that describe your actions in terms of content and intent, and the specific words contained in the messages would provide only a tiny part of the information. Finally, a third agent might have access to additional information that others do not see: a database of suspicious senders, your geographic location and local weather conditions, or a list of relatives and colleagues so that you can figure out if a message is coming from someone close to you, or finally have access to your calendar to figure out if the message arrives at a moment when you have free time.

DOI: 10.1201/9781003737339-18

In other words, some of your decisions may be completely incomprehensible to the simplest agent but easily interpreted by the most complex one. An intelligent agent understands its environment when it has a representation of it that allows it to anticipate its behavior. The same environment may be incomprehensible to one agent but perfectly understandable to another: if an agent cannot obtain an adequate representation, it can be said that the environment appears incomprehensible to it.

It is not impossible for an artificial agent to gain an understanding of some aspects of the world that are incomprehensible to us.

* * *

We are limited creatures, and for each limit, there is the possibility of being exceeded in that direction. This is true not only for our body but also for our mind, which depends on it: memory, senses, reaction times, abstraction skills, and reasoning skills. Intelligence cannot be separated from the body.

It is easy to imagine animals with better memory, senses, and reaction times than ours, and we do not take it too hard: we have gotten used to it, and we find comfort in thinking that we still have our skills of abstraction and reasoning left. My cat does not understand statistical mechanics, nor does she know what she is missing. But I wonder what she thinks of my intellectual abilities, since I do not hear the mailman coming or see the mice at the bottom of the garden. I also wonder what I am missing.

Every intelligence has limits, and so there are always territories that are inaccessible to it, while they are easily inhabited by other intelligences. It is all about deciding which abilities we want to consider most important. Intelligent machines are already capable of seeing, hearing, remembering, and reacting in ways that would be impossible for us: from hyperspectral vision to the ability to "smell" the presence of wi-fi networks, from knowing one's coordinates at any time to remembering millions of phone numbers. Even without great powers of abstraction, these superpowers alone give them a real advantage and the ability to think about the world in a completely different way than we do. But there is more.

* * *

Is it possible for an ASI to understand some aspects of the world that we cannot? Obviously, we cannot answer this by listing examples of things that transcend the human mind, so I will give only two examples to convince you that our minds are neither general nor unlimited. You will have to do the rest of the work by thinking about the different spam filters in the initial example.

Core Knowledge

The expression *core knowledge* was coined by cognitive psychologist Elizabeth Spelke and her collaborators to describe certain innate cognitive abilities of humans that form the basis of our learning and reasoning. For example, we (including infants and other primates) have innate expectations such as object permanence (the fact that objects continue to exist even when we do not see them), numerical concepts (a basic understanding of small numbers and quantities), causal reasoning (linking causes to effects), and social cognition (interpreting social signals and emotions). These assumptions are useful but not always correct and, in some cases, can mislead us. For example, we find quantum mechanics counterintuitive precisely because it does not make use of discrete objects with precise positions and connected by causal relations.

These assumptions inform the kinds of descriptions of the world we can create, just as in the initial *spam filter* example: each tool could only interpret the world in light of its own assumptions. Who knows how many things we have not yet discovered in our world because they are not describable in terms of permanent objects, local causes and effects, and numerical concepts? A different mind might describe the same world in completely different terms.

Working Memory

How many things can you keep in mind at the same time as I talk to you and the phone rings? The answer is approximately seven, at least if we go by a classic article in psychology, *The Magical Number Seven, Plus or Minus Two: Some Limits on Our Capacity for Processing Information* by George A. Miller, published in 1956. What became known as "Miller's law" says that the working (or short-term) memory of humans can hold an average of 7 ± 2 "objects," where an object can be, for example, a word, a number, or an image.

This fact greatly limits our ability to perform reasoning, where it is important to keep partial results in mind before we can come to a conclusion and places limits on the complexity of theories we can "understand." We can fully understand the solar system, where there are eight planets that hardly interact, but not the metabolic network of the human cell, where there are thousands of chemicals interacting in different ways. We can follow a movie with four protagonists, but not one with 4,000.

* * *

How could we control a super intelligence that is able to understand things that seem incomprehensible to us? This is a topic of active research, and it is not necessarily a mission impossible. A striking example comes from the story with which we opened this book: the defeat of the best human player of Go, by AlphaGo.

Seven years after defeating the human champion, an interesting experiment gave us a glimpse of what the future of coexistence with an eventual ASI might look like. In the 2023 *International Conference of Machine Learning*, a group of researchers described an algorithm designed specifically to find vulnerabilities in KataGo, one of the AlphaGo's very powerful descendants. The result was a new program for playing Go, whose game was of mediocre quality, but which had found a way to trick KataGo into making many mistakes. By exploiting that trick and the errors it induced, not only was the algorithm able to win, but human players were able to repeat the feat, repeating the moves. Although this does not seem like a true rematch, in the sense that it was another machine that defeated the AI, it perhaps teaches us a valuable lesson.

Their article states:

> *We demonstrate that even superhuman agents can be vulnerable . . . our (adversarial methods) do not win by playing a strong game of Go. Instead, they exploit blind spots in their victims. This result suggests that even highly capable agents can harbor serious vulnerabilities.*

Could this be the way we will one day control superhuman AIs?

* * *

The human mind is not universal nor unsurpassable, and there are certainly some things it cannot comprehend, even though they are understandable by a different mind. I suspect we will soon reach the boundaries of what we can know, stop there, and perhaps see our machines take a few more steps. What effect will that have on us? Maybe they will appear magical to us because they would do things incomprehensible to us, or maybe we would not care.

Do we really lose sleep because a machine plays better chess than we do?

Interlude 15. A collective enterprise.

I find it wonderful that there is a new generation of researchers dedicated to this adventure, with tools at their disposal that I could never have dreamt of during my PhD. The programming languages, the source code for the agents, the data to train them, the tests to evaluate them, the articles to study them: everything is publicly and freely available.

Today's students do not have to start from scratch every time but start exactly where their predecessors stopped: this is how we build, overcoming the "Tower of Babel," by collaborating, sharing, and participating. And this is made possible by technical as well as social and economic innovations.

The *GitHub* site, where programmers share the code they create, has billions of programs and millions of users, some of whom are entire academic or industrial labs. The Python language, which everyone now uses, is free and taught in high schools. Theoretical results are shared for free on sites created to publish scientific papers, such as *arXiv*, which contains more than two million scientific papers. The same is true for tests used in *benchmarks* and rankings: sites such as *Papers with Code* and *Hugging Face* facilitate objective comparisons between new models, and the same is true with the practice of participating in public *machine learning* competitions, on sites such as *kaggle*, where millions of users compete to solve challenges set by the research community.

The supercomputers needed for these computations are accessible "in the cloud," that is, remotely, paying only according to how many resources one has used, and there are discounts and gifts for students and academics. These are not enough to create commercially competitive models, but they are enough to test such models or to study new ones. Access to computational resources is the real point where industry has an immense advantage over academia, shortly perhaps to be joined by access to quality data.

But at least the books and journals are widely accessible for free, as are many university lectures on video, and the best international conferences: I never dreamed of that when I was in Trieste and had to wait for months for the library or the bookshop to receive *machine learning* books. And among the readers of those programs, articles and lectures are also the intelligent systems themselves, who are thus learning to program. And perhaps, they are also among the authors.

This is also how we become superhuman, that is, we transcend our individual limits: by learning to share and collaborate, creating something greater than ourselves. What I still do not see clearly is the ultimate destination: we started a journey without a map, but along the way, I expected to find one. There is still time.

16. Humanity's Last Exam

During 2025, AI evaluators prepared a final exam, which only a few exceptional individuals can pass, intended to challenge even the machines of the future. The question we will soon have to answer is: what are the limits of our intelligence?

> *Write a valid, very difficult question in English that AIs and average humans cannot answer. We aim to get questions that only exceptional individuals can answer correctly, so try and create questions that would impress you if an AI solved them. . . . Upon creating a question, we will ask state-of-the-art AI models to answer the question to help determine whether the question is too easy.*

The key words here are "average human beings" and "exceptional individuals," and this choice of terms speaks volumes. The authors of this "call for contributions" were two veteran AI evaluators, Dan Hendrycks and Alex Wang, former creators of many test batteries (including GLUE, MMLU, and MATH). Their intent is nothing less than to compare AI with the best individuals on the most difficult questions: in other words, to explore the ultimate limit of our intelligence.

By the end of 2024, the two AI researchers had decided to settle once and for all the question of which cognitive tasks were inaccessible to machines. The test they had in mind would be so difficult as to be nearly impossible even

DOI: 10.1201/9781003737339-19

for most humans, and they had called it "Humanity's Last Exam."

> *Humanity's Last Exam, [is] a project aimed at measuring how close we are to achieving expert-level AI systems. The exam is aimed at building the world's most difficult public AI benchmark gathering experts across all fields. . . . Together, we are collecting the hardest and broadest set of questions ever. Can you think of something you know that would stump current artificial intelligence (AI) systems? This will help us better evaluate the capabilities of AI systems in the years to come.*

Of course, this request carried a risk, one that both researchers must have been well aware of: all their previous *benchmarks* have been saturated by AI. To define their next test officially as the ultimate limit of human capabilities meant accepting the risk that they would in fact sanction an overtake. But the situation demanded it, especially after OpenAI's "o1" system had passed a series of difficult reasoning tests. That was the last line of defense for many evaluators. The level of ambition was also clear from the guidelines, which specified who could propose questions:

> *It's strongly encouraged that question-writers have 5+ years of experience in a technical industry job or are a PhD student or above in academic training. In preparation for Humanity's Last Exam, we found questions written by undergraduates tend to be too easy for the models. As a rough rule of thumb, if a randomly selected undergraduate can understand what is being asked, it is likely too easy for the frontier LLMs of today and tomorrow.*

The deadline for submitting questions was November 1, 2024, then a lengthy review phase would begin, to weed out all the easy questions and make sure the answers are not already on the Internet (to prevent a future AI from using them for training). The plan was to select at least 1,000 questions, to be published in 2025. Some of these will obviously be kept secret to make sure that no future AI can "know the questions before taking the exam."

What will happen next? With great optimism, the two authors say, "This will help us better evaluate the capabilities of AI systems for years to come."

The evaluators will have done their job, and it will again be time for the AI trainers to do their best to create machines that will pass this test as well. The difference from previous times is that this test is expressly designed to represent the ultimate boundaries of our intelligence: to force machines to grapple with territories that are impervious even to most humans and to ask them to compare themselves with our champions, as we had asked them to compare themselves with Lee Sedol.

It is not only a test but also inevitably a definition. And it is a challenge to our innate reluctance to concede that machines can surpass us in intelligence.[1]

note

[1] In 2026, the performance of the leading LLMs on HLE is over 64 percent, obtained by Claude Mythos.

Epilogue

One day, perhaps, the powerful mechanisms we are building will be superhuman because they will be created through the collaboration of millions of people and infused with an intelligence created from the knowledge of millions of other people, trained on millions of books and newspapers and much more.

If this happens, let us remember that it will only be intelligence, nothing more: not consciousness, emotion, free will, or volition. We humans feel strongly that we have all these things, and more, in a combination so special that it is unique and irreproducible. And even if we met a stranger who grew up in a land so far away that we did not have a single word in common, we know that we could still understand each other. None of this is intelligence, it is humanity, and it does not belong to any machine.

Experiments in recent years show a growing number of tasks in which we have been surpassed by our machines, many of which were considered signs of intelligence even recently. But we, through AI evaluators, continue to raise the challenge: "Yes, you've done that too, but . . . ."

I like that this is the case, it shows who we are: we hope against hope, we believe against all evidence, and we sometimes prefer to dream rather than see clearly. Is it not a gift to recognize our smallness in the universe, while at the same time finding deep meaning in our lives? Is this not what makes us human? To hope when there is nothing to justify it, to have faith against all logic?

This is our strength and our weakness, a blessing and a curse: imagining that there is always a better place beyond the next mountain, so we can keep going. We fight for what we cannot achieve, even though we know it. And when we lose what we love, or a dream, we deal with the pain in the same way: we deny it, we bargain with the gods, we dream of impossible ways out. And in the end, we create another dream.

We teach our children that we are special, superior to every other being, not out of arrogance, but to cultivate their strength of character, the imagination that nourishes the human spirit, and dignity. And we continue our march toward our goal, that we cannot quite name.

After his defeat by AlphaGo, champion Lee Sedol apologized "for being so weak". Let us not do that. One thing I have learned on my journey: there is nothing wrong with being weak.

Of course, we are not invincible, not even in intelligence; deep down, we have always known that. If we encounter something superior to us? We will face it with the same hope, faith, and dignified resistance.

And we will say proudly: "Yes, but . . . ."

There are more things in heaven and earth, Horatio, than are dreamt of in your philosophy.

William Shakespeare, Hamlet, *Act I, Scene V*

Informal Glossary

AI (Artificial Intelligence). The science and art of building intelligent machines, that is, capable of solving problems and making decisions in situations never previously encountered.

ANI (Artificial Narrow Intelligence). Artificial intelligence that specializes in solving a single type of problem.

AGI (Artificial General Intelligence). Hypothetical form of artificial intelligence capable of solving the same cognitive tasks as a human being, at a comparable level of competence.

ASI (Artificial Super Intelligence). Hypothetical form of artificial intelligence capable of outperforming humans in solving cognitive tasks.

Benchmark. A battery of standardized tests intended to measure the performance of an intelligent agent to facilitate objective and rigorous comparisons.

Size and scale. The word "dimensions" can be ambiguous in our context because it could refer either to the size of an AI model or to the different directions in which an agent's intelligence can develop (the different dimensions of intelligence, for example: linguistic, spatial, or mathematical). To avoid misunderstandings, where necessary we will use "scale" in the former case (e.g., small-scale models) or "cognitive dimensions" in the latter.

Language Model (Large Language Model). A type of AI designed to understand and generate natural language text. Obtained by training a neural network called a "transformer" on huge amounts of text (hundreds of billions of words). It can answer complex questions in a variety of disciplines.

Scaling Hypothesis. The conjecture that the cognitive performance of language models will increase as they scale up in size (possibly reaching and exceeding that of humans).

Validity of a psychometric test. The degree to which the test measures the psychological trait it is intended to measure (for example: introversion, depression, or language comprehension).

Psychometry. The branch of psychology that deals with the measurement of psychological characteristics of a person in an objective and rigorous manner.

Neural network. *Machine learning* algorithm inspired by the structure of the cerebral cortex, composed of a network of computational elements called neurons.

Transformer. A specific type of neural network designed to accept word sequences as input and produce word sequences as response. If trained appropriately, it can learn to translate, respond, and summarize.

Reasoning. Way of thinking that proceeds from premises to conclusions, through a series of explicit and rigorous steps.

Planning (in AI). Finding a sequence of actions that lead from an initial state to a desired goal, for example, to solve a Rubik's cube or exit a maze. Such a sequence is called a plan.

Dual System Theory. A model of human cognition that describes two ways of thinking: the first, intuitive and implicit, called System 1; and the second, reasoned and explicit, called System 2.

CHC model. Model of human cognitive abilities, described as a set of different abilities organized at three levels: some more general (such as reasoning ability) and some more specific (such as short-term memory). The abilities are divided into three levels: narrow, broad, and general. The name stands for Cattell-Horn-Carroll.

ChatGPT. Intelligent agent created by OpenAI that makes use of the GPT model, available at https://chatgpt.com/

Gemini. Intelligent agent created by Google-DeepMind that makes use of the Gemini model, available at https://gemini.google.com/

Claude. Intelligent agent making use of the Claude model created by Anthropic, available at https://claude.ai/

Llama. AI model created by Meta, not directly available as an agent for conversations, but embedded in several products, available at https://labs.perplexity.ai/

Bibliography

I.

Grother, P. *et al.*, *Face Recognition Technology Evaluation (FRTE), Part 1: Verification*, in "NIST", 2024; pages.nist.gov/frvt/reports/11/frvt_11_report.pdf

Haenssle, H.A. *et al.*, *Man against Machine: Diagnostic Performance of a Deep Learning Convolutional Neural Network for Dermoscopic Melanoma Recognition in Comparison to 58 Dermatologists*, in "Annals of Oncology", 29, 8, 2018, pp. 1836–1842.

McKinney, S.M. *et al.*, *International Evaluation of an AI System for Breast Cancer Screening*, in "Nature", 577, 7788, 2020, pp. 89–94.

Phillips, P.J. *et al.*, *Face Recognition Accuracy of Forensic Examiners, Superrecognizers, and Face Recognition Algorithms*, in "Proceedings of the National Academy of Sciences", 115, 24, 2018, pp. 6171–6176.

Rajpurkar, P., *CheXNet: Radiologist-Level Pneumonia Detection on Chest X-Rays with Deep Learning*, in "arXiv", arXiv:1711.5225, 2017.

Rumelhart, D.E., Hinton, G.E. and Williams R.J., *Learning Representations by Back-Propagating Errors*, in "Nature", 323, 6088, 1986, pp. 533–536.

Seah, J.C.Y. *et al.*, *Effect of a Comprehensive Deep-Learning Model on the Accuracy of Chest X-Ray Interpretation by Radiologists: A Retrospective, Multireader Multicase Study*, in "The Lancet Digital Health", 3, 8, 2021, pp. e496–e506.

US Food and Drug Administration, *Artificial Intelligence and Machine Learning (AI/ML)-Enabled Medical Devices*, in "AI/ML-Enabled Medical Devices", 2022; https://www.

fda.gov/medical-devices/software-medical-device-samd/artificial-intelligence-and-machine-learning-aiml-enabled-medical-devices

II.

Agüera y Arcas, B. and Norvig, P., *Artificial General Intelligence Is Already Here*, in "Noema Magazine", 2023; https://www.noemamag.com/artificial-general-intelligence-is-already-here/

Artificial Intelligence Index Report, Stanford, Stanford University, 2024; HAI_AI-Index-Report-2024.pdf (stanford.edu)

Can AI Scaling Continue through 2030?, in "Epoch AI", 2024; https://epochai.org/blog/can-ai-scaling-continue-through-2030

Claude 3.5 Sonnet, Anthropic, 2024; https://www.anthropic.com/news/claude-3-5-sonnet

Cobbe, K. *et al.*, *Training Verifiers to Solve Math Word Problems*, in "arXiv", preprint arXiv:2110.14168, 2021; arxiv.org/pdf/2110.14168

Computation Used to Train Notable AI Systems, in "Our World in Data", 2024; https://ourworldindata.org/grapher/artificial-intelligence-training-computation

Douwe, K. *et al.*, *Dynabench: Rethinking Benchmarking in NLP*, in "arXiv", preprint arXiv:2104.14337, 2021.

Dubey, A. *et al.*, *The Llama 3 Herd of Models*, in "arXiv", preprint arXiv:2407.21783, 2024.

Goertzel, B. and Cassio, P., *Artificial General Intelligence*, Berlin, Physica-Verlag, 2007.

Hendrycks, D. *et al.*, *Measuring Massive Multitask Language Understanding*, in "International Conference on Learning Representations", 2021.

Kaplan, J. *et al.*, *Scaling Laws for Neural Language Models*, in "arXiv", preprint arXiv:2001.08361, 2020.

Learning to Reason with LLMs, in "OpenAI", 2024; https://openai.com/index/learning-to-reason-with-llms/

Lohr, S., *AI Has a Math Problem*, in "The New York Times", 2024; https://www.nytimes.com/2024/07/23/technology/ai-chatbots-chatgpt-math.html

Machine Learning Trends, in "Epoch AI", 2024; https://epochai.org/trends

Metz, R., *OpenAI Scale Ranks Progress Toward 'Human-Level' Problem Solving*, Bloomberg, 2024; https://www.bloomberg.com/news/articles/2024-07-11/openai-sets-levels-to-track-progress-toward-superintelligent-ai

Nangia, N. and Bowman, S.R., *Human vs. Muppet: A Conservative Estimate of Human Performance on the GLUE Benchmark*, in "arXiv", preprint arXiv:1905.10425, 2019.

Notable AI Models, in "Epoch AI", 2024; https://epochai.org/data/notable-ai-models

Parameters in Notable Artificial Intelligence Systems, in "Our World in Data", 2024; https://ourworldindata.org/grapher/artificial-intelligence-parameter-count

Pietschnig, J. and Voracek, M., *One Century of Global IQ Gains: A Formal Meta-Analysis of the Flynn Effect (1909–2013)*, in "Perspectives on Psychological Science", 10, 3, 2015, pp. 282–306; https://doi.org/10.1177/1745691615577701

Raffel, C. *et al.*, *Exploring the Limits of Transfer Learning with a Unified Text-to-Text Transformer*, in "arXiv", arXiv:1910.10683, 2019; https://arxiv.org/abs/1910.10683

Ringel Morris, M. *et al.*, *Levels of AGI for Operationalizing Progress on the Path to AGI*, in "arXiv", arXiv:2311.02462, 2024.

The Scaling Hypothesis, in "Gwern Branwen", 2020; https://gwern.net/scaling-hypothesis

Sutton, R., *The Bitter Lesson*, 2019; http://www.incompleteideas.net/IncIdeas/BitterLesson.html

Thurstone, L.L., *Primary Mental Abilities*, Chicago, University of Chicago Press, 1938.

Valmeekam, K. *et al.*, *Planning in Strawberry Fields: Evaluating and Improving the Planning and Scheduling Capabilities of LRM o1*, in "aiXiv", arXiv:2410.02162, 2024; https://arxiv.org/pdf/2410.02162

Villalobos, P. *et al.*, *Will We Run Out of Data?*, in "aiXiv", arXiv:2410.02162, 2024; https://arxiv.org/pdf/2211.04325

Wang, A. *et al.*, *GLUE: A Multi-Task Benchmark and Analysis Platform for Natural Language Understanding*, in "arXiv", preprint arXiv:1804.07461, 2018.

Wang, A. *et al.*, *Superglue: A Stickier Benchmark for General-Purpose Language Understanding Systems*, in "Advances in Neural Information Processing Systems", 32, 2019.
Why Are Our IQ *Levels Higher Than Our Grandparents*, TED Talk, 2013; https://www.ted.com/talks/james_flynn_why_our_iq_levels_are_higher_than_our_grandparents

III.

Amodei, D., *Machines of Loving Grace How AI Could Transform the World for the Better*, 2024; https://darioamodei.com/machines-of-loving-grace
Aschenbrenner, L., *Situational Awareness: The Decade Ahead*, June 2024; https://situational-awareness.ai
CAIS (safe.ai), *Humanity's Last Exam Submission Form*; https://agi.safe.ai/submit
CAIS (safe.ai), *Submit Your Toughest Questions for Humanity's Last Exam*, 2024; https://www.safe.ai/blog/humanitys-last-exam
Dastin, J. and Paul, K., *AI Experts Ready 'Humanity's Last Exam' to Stump Powerful Tech*, 2024; https://www.reuters.com/technology/artificial-intelligence/ai-experts-ready-humanitys-last-exam-stump-powerful-tech-2024-09-16/
Github Staff, *Octoverse: AI Leads Python to Top Language as the Number of Global Developers Surges*, October 2024; https://github.blog/news-insights/octoverse/octoverse-2024/
Lopez, G. and Jackson, L., *A Deal in Hollywood*, in "The New York Times", 2023; https://www.nytimes.com/2023/09/25/briefing/writers-strike-hollywood.html
Sorgi, G., *EU Gives More Power to AI Translation Machines*, June 2023; https://www.politico.eu/article/ai-technology-eu-commission-parliament-gives-more-power-to-ai-translation-machines/
Wang, T.T. *et al.*, *Adversarial Policies Beat Superhuman Go AIs*, in "aiXiv", arXiv:2211.00241, 2023; https://proceedings.mlr.press/v202/wang23g/wang23g.pdf

www.ingramcontent.com/pod-product-compliance
Lightning Source LLC
LaVergne TN
LVHW081248151026
850117LV00029B/261
9781041232667